Doing History
from the Bottom Up

Doing History from the Bottom Up

On E. P. Thompson, Howard Zinn, and
Rebuilding the Labor Movement from Below

Staughton Lynd

Haymarket Books
Chicago, IL

First published by Haymarket Books in 2014
© 2014 Staughton Lynd

Haymarket Books
PO Box 180165
Chicago, IL 60618
773-583-7884
info@haymarketbooks.org
www.haymarketbooks.org

ISBN: 978-1-60846-388-6

Trade distribution:
In the US, through Consortium Book Sales and Distribution, www.cbsd.com
In the UK, Turnaround Publisher Services, www.turnaround-psl.com
All other countries, Publishers Group Worldwide, www.pgw.com

Special discounts are available for bulk purchases by organizations and
institutions. Please contact Haymarket Books for more information at
773-583-7884 or info@haymarketbooks.org.

This book was published with the generous support
of Lannan Foundation and the Wallace Action Fund.

Library of Congress CIP data is available.

Entered into digital printing August, 2022.

Cover photo: Staughton Lynd tape recording oral histories
at the Writers' Worskhop in Gary, Indiana, 1971.

Contents

Foreword
Staughton Lynd and "Doing History"
Edward Countryman

Almost half a century ago Staughton Lynd published his first collection of essays, *Class Conflict, Slavery, and the United States Constitution*. English historian E. P. (Edward) Thompson, who (together with Howard Zinn) figures strongly in these pages, contributed the book's foreword. Edward did not claim to know American historiography. But he spotted in Staughton a serious fellow practitioner of hard research, careful reasoning about what the research revealed, and caring about what difference knowing history makes.

By the time he published *Class Conflict*, Staughton had gained fame for his commitment to civil rights and his opposition to the war in Vietnam. Despite his academic record (which included being one of the few historians to write a master's essay that deserved publication as a book), Staughton's politics were too much for the administrators at Yale, who denied him tenure. This was shortly after Edward joined the University of Warwick, which drove him out for political reasons five years after *Class Conflict* appeared in print.

Outside the academy, their paths seemed to diverge. Thanks to Dorothy Thompson's position at the University of Birmingham and to visits both of them made to American campuses, Edward was able to keep writing at a furious pace, producing fine historical work and a huge body of political commentary. He gained world fame as an opponent of the Reagan-Thatcher-Brezhnev nuclear buildup, when supposedly responsible statesmen and planners were talking about "survivable" nuclear war.

I was among a quarter-million people who heard him in London's Hyde Park. I remember a half-facetious sign on that demonstration that read "Historians Against the Bomb: We Demand a Continuing Supply of History." Edward could be contentious, and he quarreled as strongly with notable supposed allies as he did with outright political opponents. His death in 1993 was front-page and prime-time UK news.

Staughton went to law school, not with the goal of making a lot of money but with the clear realization that there was practical hard work to do among and for working people in what used to be the American republic's industrial heartland and now is its Rust Belt. When he and Alice Lynd retired from employment as lawyers in 1996, they turned their attention to the obscenity that is the American prison system. Though they are in their eighties, they have not let up to this day, most recently taking on the cause of hunger strikers at Menard Correctional Center in Southern Illinois, where, it happens, I call one of the inmates my friend.

But like Edward Thompson, Staughton Lynd continued to write. *Doing History* is the *thirtieth* book that he has written, cowritten, or edited. I first encountered his writing at Manhattan College, thanks to my teacher Bob Christen, who had been Staughton's graduate school colleague at Columbia and who amassed his own superb record in the public sphere. (In my naiveté I was amazed to see Staughton thanking Bob in the preface to his master's essay.) But I did not meet Staughton until a remarkable group of historians interested in American radicalism gathered at a dude ranch in Montana early in this millennium. Long-ago colaborers in early American history writing were there, most notably Alfred F. Young, and so were younger scholars. Al encouraged Staughton to return to a manuscript he had set aside when his academic life ended, which Staughton and historian David Waldstreicher published together in the prestigious *William and Mary Quarterly*.Exile and blacklisting need not be forever.

But Staughton never acted like an exile. He left the academy, but he went on "doing" history in all senses of this book's title. He did history by making it with the cases that he and Alice took to court. He did history by observing others make it: the people all around him who were struggling against the rolling destruction that impersonal corporations were wreaking on lives, jobs, communities, and a whole way of life across the industrial American Midwest. He did history by gathering their stories so that the record of what happened and what working people thought, said, and did while most of the American steel industry was being gutted would be preserved. He did history by pondering what he was learning from them. He does history in all of these senses in the long second part of this book.

What he writes is not just the story of what happened as Big Steel went down in Youngstown and during the Little Steel struggles in Indiana. It's also a reflection on what was possible, in terms that go beyond the usual stuff of labor history. The field currently is unfashionable; it badly needs to come back to life. That's partly for the sake of understanding how industrial capitalist America has given way to the onslaught of service, information, and high-finance capitalist America, where the needs, powers, and utter lack of social responsibility on the part of corporations seem to know no limit. But it's also for the sake of asking what is to be done, particularly in view of what the mainstream unions have and have not done, can and cannot do on behalf of the people who make them up. He presents a searing indictment not only of often self-serving union leadership but of the whole structure of labor-management relations that took shape during the New Deal.

That structure, centered on contracts and the National Labor Relations Board, has been under a ferocious onslaught ever since Ronald Reagan broke the strike of air traffic controllers early in his first presidential term. The onslaught continues. Boeing has taken advantage of the legal inability of the International Association of Machinists to strike while a contract is in force, in order to impose poorer conditions on new workers on its 777 production line in Seattle. Republican politicians in Tennessee have deployed outright threats against both Volkswagen and its Chattanooga workforce to defeat an organizing drive by the United Auto Workers. Behemoth retailers including (but not limited to) Walmart, Whole Foods, Amazon.com, and the whole fast-food sector make enormous efforts to keep unions out of their stores and their gargantuan warehouses.

Staughton does not attack the post–New Deal history of American unions as an enemy but with a mind on the question, what is to be done? Lenin posed the problem famously, and his answer was the Bolshevik model of a revolutionary party, whatever actual Russian workers proposed. Historians cannot *not* give an answer to such a question. We make spectacularly poor prophets. We have enough trouble understanding whatever did happen. The crystal balls of economists frequently prove no better.

But Staughton's reflections in these pages command attention. His subjects are people facing, thinking about, and dealing with the conditions of their lives for the sake of a better future. From Staughton's earliest study of tenant farmers in revolutionary-era New York to this book, his interest has lain with what they did think and did do, sometimes winning, often not. Central to this book is what American working men and working women have done in the face of enormous corporate and political power, based on *their* clear understanding of how the present got to be what it is. Only on that basis is there any possibility of shaping the kind of future that they want, different from the present because it is better, not worse.

That is as much as a working historian can "do." But doing history means making it as well as researching and writing it. In the tradition of Edward Thompson and Howard Zinn, Staughton Lynd has been doing history in multiple ways over his whole lifetime.

Preface and Acknowledgments

During the past several years we have lost David Montgomery, Alfred Young, and Howard Zinn. In different ways they all practiced what Jesse Lemisch long ago christened "history from the bottom up."

There has been vigorous debate among historians concerning Howard's *People's History*. Most of the critiques were launched after his death, when he could no longer respond.[1] Apart from swordplay with such critics, those of us who continue to practice history from below need to clarify what we are doing so as to focus our efforts and assist each other more effectively.

Let me begin by offering three proposed perspectives.

1. History from below is not, or should not be, mere description of hitherto invisible poor and oppressed people: it should challenge mainstream versions of the past.

In words that I have repeatedly quoted, Thomas Humphrey has written that historians who do history from below "have heretofore only succeeded in pressing the authors of the master narrative, which largely ignores class and class struggle, to alter their stories slightly or, worse, to add another box for 'the poor' on the margins" of the page.[2]

To say the same thing in a different way, currently fashionable history will give us the franchise for chimneysweeps who get cancer and seamstresses who burn to death when the foreman locks the door, so long as we do not challenge the belief that American history is an exceptional story that other nations should do their best to imitate.

It may well be that we should consider whether this nation's history is "exceptional." But we must be open to that inquiry leading in more than one direction. For example, one might ask: were mainland British colonies and Haiti exceptional among colonies in the Western Hemisphere in requiring a bloody civil war to abolish slavery?

2. The United States was founded on crimes against humanity directed at Native Americans and African American slaves.

Why do we condemn those who stood by and did nothing in the 1930s and 1940s, while inventing endless nuanced explanations for the behavior of white Americans in the 1780s and thereafter? May 1787, the month in which the Constitutional Convention assembled in Philadelphia, was also the month in which a small group of men meeting in London founded what would become the British movement to end the slave trade. James Madison's notes on the meetings of the Constitutional Convention make clear that participants knew slavery to be morally wrong. It is not anachronistic to insist that eighteenth-century Americans could have done much more toward the abolition of slavery.

A number of terms suggest themselves to describe what white European settlers did to brown human beings whom they found in the New World and to black human beings whom they imported to be slaves. *Holocaust* and *genocide* denote the deliberate murder of populations.[3] But slaves were imported for their labor, and Native Americans were exterminated or forcibly transferred to reservations so that white settlers could take their land.

"Crime against the peace," one of the crimes identified by the Nuremburg Tribunal, applies when a country that has not been attacked starts a war. "War crimes," a second category of crimes defined at Nuremburg, refers to actions committed during the course of a war. I believe the best term to define the original sins of our new nation is the third kind of crime conceptualized at Nuremburg: "crimes against humanity."

As defined by Principle VI of the Nuremburg Principles, crimes against humanity are

> Murder, extermination, enslavement, deportation and other inhuman acts done against any civilian population, or persecutions on political, racial or religious grounds, when such acts are done or such persecutions are carried on in execution of or in connection with any crime against peace or any war crime.

The crimes of "extermination," "enslavement," and "deportation" appear accurately to describe much of the early history of the United States.

Al Young, Jesse Lemisch, and I concentrated our research on the experience of poor, but for the most part Caucasian, colonists. Al told in marvelous detail the stories of a Boston shoemaker and of a woman who became a soldier in the War for Independence by disguising herself as a man. Jesse focused on sailors, most of whom were white (although some, like Crispus Attucks, were African Americans). I studied Hudson Valley tenants and New York City artisans. We suggested that many sailors, tenant farmers, and artisans stood up against British imperialism before bewigged gentlemen in knee breeches became part of the independence movement. Sailors resisted British impressment in the streets of New England in the 1750s, and the leader of a 1766 tenant uprising in New York was sentenced to be hanged, drawn, and quartered for treason. The first conclusion of a 2011 volume that Al helped to edit is "Common farmers, artisans, and laborers often led the resistance to imperial policies. [They] moved the American Revolution in some direction the traditional founders did not want to take, extending it farther and deeper than a separation from the British Empire. They made the Revolution more revolutionary."[4]

But for people of color it was otherwise. I do not claim expertise regarding either Native Americans or slaves, but there does not appear to be serious disagreement among historians about the facts. Native Americans desperately tried to determine which group of whites was least likely to steal their land. Different tribes made different choices: the Revolution divided the Cherokees and gave rise to civil war within the Iroquois confederacy. The Oneidas supported the Revolution, but the "grabbing of Oneida lands continued at a frenetic pace."[5]

As for slaves, it is true that over a period of decades the Northern states initiated various versions of gradual emancipation, but to say only this misrepresents what happened. As I have argued elsewhere,[6] the Continental Congress and the Constitutional Convention, meeting ninety miles apart in the summer of 1787, opened the Southwest to the expansion of slavery. There were about 600,000 slaves in the thirteen colonies at the time of the Revolution. Some fought the British, but more fled to the British in response to promises of freedom. By the time of the Civil War, enslaved African Americans in the United States numbered approximately four million.

Thus seen from what is truly "the bottom up," there was little to celebrate about the War for Independence.

3. Participants in making history should be regarded not only as sources of facts but as colleagues in interpreting what happened.

In the practice of guerrilla history the insights of nonacademic protagonists are considered to be potentially as valuable as those of the historian. Thus guerrilla history is not a process wherein the poor and oppressed provide poignant facts and a radical academic interprets them. Historical agent and professor of history are understood to be coworkers, together mapping out the terrain traveled and the possibility of openings in the mountain ridges ahead.

Herein I offer steelworker John Sargent as an example of one who, personally involved but without academic credentials, understood what happened better than commentators external to the experience, indeed turned the conventional interpretation upside down.

Nick Turse's deservedly applauded book about the Vietnam War, *Kill Anything That Moves*, also had its origins in history perceived from below. The truth of what happened at My Lai, Turse writes, "might have remained hidden forever if not for the perseverance of a single Vietnam veteran named Ron Ridenhour." Ridenhour was not in My Lai on the day of the massacre there but "heard about the slaughter from other soldiers." He then took "the unprecedented step of carefully gathering testimonies from multiple American witnesses." Similarly, medical corpsman Jamie Henry "stepped forward and reported the crimes he'd seen." Turce might also have mentioned helicopter pilot Hugh Thompson and his crew, who, watching in horror what was happening on the ground below them in My Lai, landed, trained their weapons on fellow soldiers, and safely evacuated several elderly men and women and (as I count them) six children.[7]

A final example of the protagonist as historian is Leon Trotsky. Surprisingly, the former Bolshevik military commander accurately perceived an event in which that vanguard party played no role at all. Describing the uprising that overthrew the czar, Trotsky wrote: "The fact is that the February [1917] revolution was begun from below, overcoming the resistance of its own revolutionary organizations, the initiative being taken of their own accord by the most oppressed and downtrodden part of the proletariat—the women textile workers, among them no doubt many soldiers' wives."[8]

The term *guerrilla history* refers to narratives by such persons who took part in the events they are describing. But guerrilla history is only one part of the larger project of doing history from below. We must be wary of the notion that anything participants believe about their history is necessarily true. A good example occurs at the very beginning of Frank Bardacke's *Trampling Out the Vintage*, a history of the United Farm Workers union. Frank asked two friends with whom he had driven to work in the fields and who had performed decades of farm work in California what had caused the union to "get beat." One thought it was the election of a new California governor. The other was sure the union had been sold out by a trusted *gabacho* (a derogatory term for an Anglo). Frank reluctantly concluded that both these interpretations from below were superficial and unsatisfactory, and ventured forth on his own.[9]

My wife Alice Lynd and I have struggled with a similar problem in working with prisoners. As to some crucial issues concerning the Lucasville prison uprising of 1993, we have agreed to disagree with certain of the death-sentenced defendants while together pursuing "discovery" that will hopefully settle the matter.

Protagonists' perceptions of their own history need to be corroborated, when possible, by the testimony of other witnesses and by independent objective evidence, including written sources. Nevertheless, the perceptions of poor people who were present in the flesh, at the time, should be the starting point for history from below. Viktor Frankl puts it this way at the outset of his book on Auschwitz and other concentration camps:

> [D]oes a man who makes his observations while he himself is a prisoner possess the necessary detachment? Such detachment is granted to the outsider, but he is too far removed to make any statements of real value. Only the man inside knows. His judgments may not be objective; his evaluations may be out of proportion. This is inevitable. An attempt must be made to avoid any personal bias, and that is the real difficulty.[10]

This Book

This little book seeks clarification of history from below in two parts.

Part I offers commentaries on the work of two mentors and exemplars, Edward Thompson and Howard Zinn.

Part II describes my own work in probing the decline of trade unionism in the United States during a quarter-century in which I pursued this project both as historian and as lawyer, together with some thoughts about what hope there may be for reversing that decline. Of all the subjects about which I have written or might write, labor history has engaged me the longest, in a three-dimensional interplay of oral history, documentary research, and active involvement in trying to make things happen. Hence that story seems to be the one I need to try to tell.

But because I have played the part of an observant participant, not merely a participant observer, my involvement presents the question raised by Frankl of whether I am sufficiently free from bias to write truthful and reliable history. As I perceive my own work, I have faithfully sought to discern what Leopold Ranke called *wie es eigentlich gewesen* (how it really happened). Repeatedly I have found myself puzzled by unexpected evidence that forced me to revise an initial hypothesis.

Finally, the question of working-class solidarity (or the absence thereof) is central for me. Some authors celebrate the mutual aid of persons who depend on the informal economy. The comradeship of soldiers, helping each other to survive a war in which they no longer believe, also demands attention. But the reciprocal accompaniment of those who work together seems to me the element without which it is difficult to imagine a future.

A critical follow-up question concerns whether the more than two million individuals presently imprisoned in the United States should be considered part of the working class. Imagine what the unemployment rate might amount to if prisoners were included in the tally of those without work!

Spokespersons for prisoners in California held in indefinite solitary confinement declared, in suspending their sixty-day hunger strike in 2013, that they were members of "the working class poor warehoused in prisons."[11] One of the drafters of the statement (a white man) explained in a letter to me:

> I've been having some dialogue with various men up here regarding [our] need to shift our mentality from a focus on race—because such is a form of divisiveness and we are all similarly situated, subject to very hard times, poor prospects, etc., etc., irregardless of race!

He continued:

> It's a class war people can no longer ignore. . . . A microcosm of the working-class poor is the "prisoner class," and until people come together—across racial lines—collectively, for the benefit of all similarly situated people, we will not be effective!

This correspondent concluded:

> We need to have awareness of, and respect for, the differences of

the races—historically, culturally, and presently people of color have been and are still subject to racist policies and practices!!

It's also true that poor whites are getting more of the short end each day. The line between the two [races, black and white] is blurring!

The powers that be need the two to remain at odds—divided, distrustful, and warring with each other. They manipulate continued conflict the same way they do in these prisons!!

Because they know a unified people is a mighty force that can halt the elitist agenda![12]

I wish to thank a few of the many people who have encouraged me (some without knowing that they were doing so) to persist in trying to untangle these matters: Jeremy Brecher, Alexis Buss, Charlie Cobb, Vaneesa Cook, Edward Countryman, Robin Einhorn, Erik Forman, Daniel Gross, Andrej Grubacic, Wesley Hogan, Thomas Humphrey, Noel Ignatiev, Diane Krauthamer, Glorianne Leck, Jesse Lemisch, Jules Lobel, Alice Lynd, Charlie McCollester, Eric O'Neil, Andy Piascik, Marcus Rediker, David Roediger, Thomas Sabatini, Mike Stout, Lorry Swain, Michael Vorenberg, David Waldstreicher, and Mark Weber; as well as my granddaughter and historian-to-be Hilary Rybeck Lynd, to whom I dedicate this book.

Credits

All the essays that follow have been published previously with the exception of the multi-segment essay on Howard Zinn. A very few changes have been made to correct errors, a few passages that now seem of lesser importance have been omitted, and in some cases footnotes have been condensed. Permission to reprint has kindly been granted as follows:

- "In Memoriam: E. P. Thompson," from *Living inside Our Hope: A Steadfast Radical's Thoughts on Rebuilding the Movement*, copyright 1997 by Cornell University, is used by permission of the publisher, Cornell University Press.

- "Edward Thompson's Warrens" and "Guerrilla History in Gary" previously appeared in *From Here to There: The Staughton Lynd Reader*, ed. Andrej Grubacic (Oakland, CA: PM Press, 2010) and are reprinted with permission.

- The extracts from "Your Dog Don't Bark No More" appear in *Rank and File: Personal Histories by Working-Class Organizers*, ed. Alice and Staughton Lynd, expanded ed. (Chicago: Haymarket Books, 2011).

- "Plant Closing: Local 1330 v. U.S. Steel (1997–1980)" appeared in *American Labor Struggles and Law Histories*, ed. Kenneth M. Casebeer (Durham, NC: Carolina Academic Press, 2011) and is reprinted with permission.

- "The Possibility of Radicalism in the Early 1930s: The Case of Steel" is reprinted with permission from *Workers' Struggles, Past and Present: A "Radical America" Reader*, ed. James Green (Philadelphia: Temple University Press, 1983).

- "'We Are All We've Got': Building a Retiree Movement in Youngstown, Ohio," by Alice Lynd and Staughton Lynd, is reprinted with permission from *Law Stories*, ed. Gary Bellow and Martha Minow (Ann Arbor: University of Michigan Press, 1996).

- Part of chapter 3 of *Solidarity Unionism: Rebuilding the Labor Movement from Below*, titled "Is There an Alternative to the Unionism We Have Now?," is republished with the permission of the Charles H. Kerr Publishing Company.

- The introduction to *"We Are All Leaders": The Alternative Unionism of the Early 1930s*, copyright 1996 by the Board of Trustees of the University of Illinois, is used with permission of the University of Illinois Press.

Part I
Mentors and Exemplars

Introduction

What do I mean by calling E. P. Thompson and Howard Zinn "mentors and exemplars"?

First and most obviously, the Brits were earlier in time. All of us who started to do history from below in the United States in the early 1960s were inspired by British pioneers like E. P. Thompson and Christopher Hill. The single most important book to play this role was Edward Thompson's *The Making of the English Working Class*.

A major Thompson theme was that poor and working people initiate and act—to use a favorite word of Thompson's, display "agency"—in confronting the difficult circumstances of their lives. The agency of working people has to do with "the degree by which they contributed, by conscious efforts, to the making of history." To portray them as suffering but inert would be to exhibit "the enormous condescension of posterity."[1]

Agency is one of four terms I have encountered by means of which Left intellectuals seek to describe roughly the same thing. Here are the other three:

1. *Self-activity.* Jesse Lemisch has remarked that "self-activity" is a term used by C. L. R. James and the people around him, such as George Rawick.[2]

2. *Samodeyatelnost.* This is Russian for "self-activity." Leon Trotsky and Alexandra Kollontai both used the word *samodeyatelnost* to distinguish the self-activity of workers and working women that they championed from Lenin's model of a vanguard party.[3]

3. *Autogestion.* This word, according to historian Jay Winter, arose "out of 1968" and may be "variously interpreted as

local self-government, collective self-management on
the local or factory level, or workers' control." From this
platform, he continues, "emerged the social movements of
the 1980s and 1990s." Versions of *autogestion* appeared in
the Israeli kibbutzim and among trade unionists in Tito's
Yugoslavia, as well as in Peru and Algeria. Three elements
stand out, according to Winter: a commitment to the
decentralization of political and social life; a demand for
local autonomy in all places of work and public service;
and "a vision of the replacement of the capitalist organization of consumption by cooperative institutions."[4]

In this international context, Thompson and Zinn functioned as
what Antonio Gramsci termed "organic intellectuals," who combined
theory and practice in a manner atypical among full-time academics.
The same was true of others like Stan Weir (who worked as a sailor, as a
longshoreman, and on an assembly line before helping to create a small
publishing house, Singlejack Books), Marty Glaberman (who, after
years of working in automobile plants, wrote a book on wildcat strikes
during World War II and became a distributor of the writings of C. L.
R. James), Frank Bardacke (who taught English as a second language in
Watsonville, a farmworker center, while assembling his history of the
United Farm Workers), and myself (who became a lawyer and with this
credential moved to a steel town, Youngstown, Ohio).

Thompson and Zinn exemplified the meaning of the term "organic intellectual" in different ways. Thompson wrote his greatest book while serving a workers' education program in the North of England as a traveling
instructor. He tried to root his historiography among graduate students at
Warwick University, but failed, and returned to life away from academia.

Zinn, perhaps because of his working-class background and strong
sense of connection with the world outside the academy, managed to be
at the same time both a full-time college professor and an activist who
coordinated campus picket lines, testified in court on behalf of protesters who defied the authorities, and on occasion was himself arrested.[5]
When I arrived at Spelman College with a dissertation still to write, I
asked Howard what scholarly papers he was preparing for which academic conferences. He looked at me as if I were speaking an unknown
foreign language. He was one of two persons (the other was Ella Baker)
who had been asked to serve as older advisers to the Student Nonviolent
Coordinating Committee.

E. P. Thompson:
In Memoriam

And did those feet in ancient time,

Walk upon England's mountains green;

And was the holy Lamb of God,

On England's pleasant pastures seen!

And did the Countenance Divine,

Shine forth upon our clouded hills?

And was Jerusalem builded here,

Among these dark Satanic mills?

Bring me my Bow of burning gold:

Bring me my Arrows of desire:

Bring me my Spear: Oh clouds unfold!

Bring me my Chariot of fire!

I will not cease from Mental Fight,

Nor shall my Sword sleep in my hand:

Till we have built Jerusalem,

In England's green & pleasant Land.

—William Blake, Preface to *Milton* (1804)

I had only one conversation with Edward Thompson. It was in the spring of 1966, at the apartment of Eugene Genovese in Manhattan. A few hours before I had been in London, speaking at a rally against the war in Vietnam. I believe I introduced myself to Edward Thompson by offering greetings from the pigeons in Trafalgar Square.

Four things from that conversation remain in my mind. Thompson spoke with disdain of historians who, in his phrase, "never untied a bundle" of manuscripts. I formed a mental picture of bundle upon bundle of manuscripts at the British Home Office, each tied with string. Be that as it may, the message was clear. Radical historians may make political demands of themselves over and above the requirements of good historical scholarship, but the requirements of historical scholarship are the same for everybody. We have to be good craftspersons, whatever else we may be.

Second, I said something to the effect that it might be the Third World, rather than the working class of advanced industrial societies, that took the lead in the transition from capitalism to socialism. Had it been a year or two later I might have cited Frantz Fanon or Regis Debray. In 1966, I believe I referred to Sartre.

Thompson reacted sharply. He did not believe for a moment that the industrial working class was finished as an historical agent. Why, there was this strike and that struggle that had just happened in Britain, and he felt sure there was more to come.

I recall being very surprised. The message to be drawn from this exchange, I think, was not that anyone could say with confidence what the respective roles of First and Third World proletariats would be in the long run; it was simply that one ought not to give up on the workers of one's own country. I apparently was influenced. I have spent the past twenty-five years as a historian and a lawyer trying to do what Thompson suggested. My clients have typically been discharged or displaced industrial workers.

A third point Thompson made in our 1966 conversation had to do with what he called "doing history" and "doing politics." He did not see how one could do both at the same time. He suggested then, and his later life seems to exemplify, that one must do history and politics in alternation, for separate periods of time.

I find this idea inadequate. Surely it falls short of what Marx called a unity of theory and practice. I wonder if the difficulty Thompson found in connecting theory and practice was related to something else: that the focus of his scholarly inquiry shifted further and further back in time, from William Morris (late nineteenth century), to the formation of the English working class (early nineteenth century), to studies in seventeenth- and eighteenth-century popular culture.

Finally, there was the question of Edward's acerbic dialogue with Perry Anderson and other British Marxists (about which I say more below). I cannot remember what point this exchange had reached at the time I spoke with Thompson in 1966. Nor can I recall any particular words that Thompson used. What came through and what stays in mind is the passion with which he spoke. Thompson's biographer Bryan Palmer describes his attitude as follows:

> Though retaining from Marxism a set of central questions and analytical methods, Thompson conceived of himself less and less in terms of traditional Marxism and more and more in terms of a moral agenda that turned on opposition to power and its abuses. "We need, in some new form," he would write in The Nation in 1983, "a 'Wobbly' vocabulary of mutual aid and plain duty to each other in the face of power."

Academic Blindness

Edward Thompson, the most influential historian writing in the English language during the second half of the twentieth century, never received a PhD. He wrote his masterpiece, *The Making of the English Working Class*, while serving as a sort of adjunct professor at a provincial university; the book was originally to be an introductory essay for a text to be used in his workers' education classes. In 1965 Thompson was appointed to a regular academic position at Warwick University, and for years I have wondered if I erred in turning down an invitation to join him there on a one-year basis. Now I learn from Edward's obituaries that in 1970 he became involved with students who had invaded the university offices and held a sit-in, and in 1971 he resigned, after writing stingingly about the ethos and administrative arrangements of this new "business university." Thereafter, until his death, Thompson lived as an independent writer and peace agitator supported in part by the academic income of his wife, Dorothy Thompson.

Thompson's life accordingly should challenge us to consider the relationship between academic livelihood and intellectual life on the Left. Perhaps more particularly, we may wonder if some of Thompson's originality and incisiveness arose precisely because he was not, during most of his life, a university professor.

For Thompson, academic custom often ran counter to the values that meant most to him. He believed in human agency, as opposed to any form of determinism; in the rationality and dignity of working people; and in the necessity of moral values and moral choices. By contrast, academic life tended to segregate teachers from practice; to persuade them that they were better than ordinary people; and to lead to amoral and sterile theorizing.

An early and much-quoted passage from "Outside the Whale" (1960) sounded Thompson's theme of human agency. During the confining years of the Cold War, Thompson wrote,

> [M]en had abandoned human agency. They could not hold back change; but change went with the shuffling gait of circumstance. It did not stem from the operation of human consciousness and will upon circumstances. Events seemed to will men, not men events. For meaning can be given to history only in the quarrel between "ought" and "is"—we must thrust the "ought" of choice into the "is" of circumstance which in its turn defines the human nature with which we choose.

Likewise, in *The Making of the English Working Class*, Thompson said it was a study "in an active process, which owes as much to agency as to conditioning," and criticized prevailing orthodoxies that "tend to obscure the agency of working people." He insisted that the poor be remembered as protagonists, as thinking men and women guided by norms of their own. In rioting for food in the eighteenth century, or in smashing machines in the early nineteenth century, those who took direct action had in mind a "legitimizing notion." They were the champions of a "moral economy" derived in part from late medieval English laws that sought to ensure access to good wheat bread at reasonable prices or to maintain the quality of English textiles. As these laws were evaded and ignored, the poor turned first to others to enforce them, but if the Justice and Parliament refused to act, they took matters into their own hands. Against academics of Right *and* Left who wished to reduce culturally mediated behavior to economics, Thompson counterposed an anthropological view, claiming that these common folk displayed "a pattern of behavior of which a Trobriand islander need not have been ashamed."

The themes of agency, working-class rationality and dignity, and the need for moral values are summoned as prosecutors of the academic way of life in "The Poverty of Theory." The essay confronts academic intellectuals who (according to Thompson) are the product of a rupture "between intellectuality and practical experience." It attacks the "characteristic delusion of intellectuals, who suppose that ordinary mortals are stupid." Further,

I must remind a Marxist philosopher that knowledges have been and still are formed outside the academic procedures. Nor have these been, in the test of practice, negligible. They have assisted men and women to till the fields, to construct houses, to support elaborate social organisations, and even, on occasion, to challenge effectively the conclusions of academic thought.

Thompson reached out to popular culture, even to religion, as an antidote to two-dimensional academicism. It is "profoundly important that our protestant prejudice should be renewed, that we should *think* ourselves to be 'free.'" The Marxism of "closure," which he deplores, has arisen and been replicated "not in the Soviet Union, but in an advanced intellectual culture in the West. Its characteristic location has been in universities." A merely theoretical Marxism "allows the aspirant academic to engage in harmless revolutionary psycho-drama, while at the same time pursuing a reputable and conventional intellectual career." Rather than be that kind of Marxist, Thompson exclaims, "I would rather be a Christian (or hope to have the courage of a certain kind of Christian radical). At least I would then be given back a vocabulary within which moral choices are allowed."

Morris, Blake, and Love

In a 1976 postscript to a new edition of his biography of William Morris (first published in 1955), Thompson went further than before in delimiting the proper scope of Marxist theory. It should now be clear, runs the crucial paragraph,

that there is a sense in which Morris, as a Utopian and moralist, can never be assimilated to Marxism, not because of any contradiction of purposes but because one may not assimilate desire to knowledge, and because the attempt to do so is to confuse two different operative principles of culture. . . . Marxism requires . . . a sense of humility before those parts of culture which it can never order. The motions of desire may be legible in the text of necessity, and may then become subject to rational explanation and criticism. But such criticisms can scarcely touch these motions at their source. "Marxism," on its own, we now know, has never made anyone "good" or "bad." . . . So what Marxism might do, for a change, is sit on its own head a little in the interest of socialism's heart. It might close down one counter in its universal pharmacy, and cease dispensing potions of analysis to cure the maladies of desire. This might do good

politically as well, since it would allow a little space . . . for the
unprescribed initiatives of ordinary men and women.

William Blake was the one radical intellectual about whom Thompson had no such mixed feelings. To begin with, unlike John Thelwall and Brontierre O'Brien, both sons of merchants, or William Morris, whose father made his fortune in mining stocks, Blake's father and brother were hosiers, as was the first husband of his mother, Catherine Hermitage. Thus Blake "straddled two social worlds: that of intellectuals and artists, and that of tradesmen and artisans."

Moreover, Thompson saw Blake as the last English intellectual at home both in working-class resistance to industrial capitalism and in the Romantic critique of Utilitarianism. Thompson's admiration for Blake, now poignantly available in the posthumously published *Witness against the Beast: William Blake and the Moral Law*, is very closely tied to his view of academic culture and his convictions about the limitations of theory.

> Despite every precaution, we have a continuing difficulty in our approach to Blake, which derives from our tendency to make overly academic assumptions as to his learning and mode of thought. It takes a large effort to rid ourselves of these assumptions, because they lie at an inaccessible level within our own intellectual culture—indeed, they belong to the very institutions and disciplines with which we construct that culture. That is, we tend to find that a man is either "educated" or "uneducated," or is educated to certain levels (within a relatively homogeneous hierarchy of attainments); and this education involves submission to certain intellectually defined disciplines, with their own hierarchies of accomplishment and authority.
>
> Blake's mind was formed within a very different intellectual tradition. In the nineteenth century we sometimes call this, a little patronizingly, the tradition of the autodidact. This calls to mind the radical or Chartist journalist, lecturer or poet, attaining by his own efforts a knowledge of "the classics." This is not right for Blake. For a great deal of the most notable intellectual energies of the eighteenth century lay outside of formal academic channeling.

The particular nonacademic intellectual tradition in which Thompson seeks to place Blake is a small but persistent Protestant sect, the Muggletonians. Like the Quakers, the Muggletonians were antinomians: that is, they believed in an "inner light" that enabled ordinary men and women to find ultimate spiritual truth, without the mediation of any externally defined moral law. Unlike the Quakers, Muggletonians refused "submission to the rationalism and civilizing modes of the time, with an accompanying upward drift in the social status of their following," and maintained their plebeian character into the second half of the eighteenth century.

Blake's supposed link with the Muggletonians derives from the fact that a man with the same last name as Blake's mother (Hermitage), who lived in the same London parish where the Blakes lived, wrote Muggletonian songs of praise. On this foundation Thompson erects the following hypothesis:

> We could suppose that William Blake in his childhood was made familiar with the structure of antinomian thought and the central images of Genesis and Revelation in a Muggletonian notation; that he turned sharply away from this in his teens, rejecting the know-all dogmatism of the sect, and its philistinism toward all the arts (except divine songs), read widely, and entered the artistic world without restraint; took stock of works of the Enlightenment; was led back toward his origins by reading Boehme and Swedenborg; and then, in his early thirties (the years of the Songs and the Marriage of Heaven and Hell) composed a symbolic world for himself in which the robust tradition of artisan and tradesman antinomianism reasserted itself, not as literal doctrines, but as a fund of imaginative possibilities and as intellectual footholds for an anti-Enlightenment stance.

The critical affirmation in Blake's intelligent anti-intellectualism, Thompson says, was love. His antinomian heritage

> enabled Blake to question and resist the simplicities of mechanical materialism and Lockean epistemology, in which the revolutionary impulse was to founder. For in shedding the prohibitives of the Moral Law, Blake held fast to the affirmative: Thou Shalt Love.

And:

> Hence Blake, however close he is to Painites, will not dispense with "The Divine Image" and the "Everlasting Gospel." Just as with deism or atheism, he can agree with the analysis but still require, at the end of it, a utopian leap. . . . To create the New Jerusalem something must be brought in from outside the ra-

tionalist system, and that something could only be found in the non-rational image of Jesus, in the affirmatives of Mercy, Pity, Peace and Love.

And last:

> The busy perfectionists and benevolent rationalists of 1791–6 nearly all ended up, by the later 1800s, as disenchanted men. Human nature, they decided, had let them down and proved stubborn in resistance to enlightenment. But William Blake, by denying even in the Songs of Experience a supreme societal value to rationality, did not suffer from the same kind of disenchantment. His vision had not been into the rational government of man but into the liberation of an unrealized potential, an alternative nature, within man.

The practice of love and solidarity by working people emerges as E. P. Thompson's great theme. The early nineteenth century experienced "the loss of any felt cohesion in the community, save that which the working people, in antagonism to their labor and their masters, built for themselves." At the end of the nineteenth century, the "social sense" had been "[b]rought near to extinction everywhere except in the centers of working-class life." Thompson valued the working class no less than did Karl Marx. But in the end the working class mattered, not because it was destined to overthrow capitalism, but because it kept alive among Satanic Mills an ethic of mutuality that prefigured a better society.

Thompson perceived the *problem* as capitalism and imperialism but the *answer* as mutual aid, plain duty to each other, building community, and creating a culture of solidarity within the shell of the old society. The special responsibility of anyone who wishes to carry on the work of Edward Thompson, it seems to me, is to seek in our own time, in whatever places we live and labor, to nurture the spirit of working-class solidarity.

Edward Thompson's Warrens[1]

The problem of the transition from capitalism to socialism has nagged at and puzzled me all my adult life.

As a high school student I pursued my political education during the half-hour trip to school on the New York City subway. I devoured Edmund Wilson's *To the Finland Station*. I read Ignazio Silone's *Bread and Wine*, still my favorite novel. And I also read a book by an ex-Trotskyist named James Burnham, *The Managerial Revolution*.

Burnham argued that the bourgeois revolution occurred only after a long period during which bourgeois institutions had been built within feudal society. The position of the proletariat within capitalist society, he contended, was altogether different. The proletariat has no way to begin to create socialist economic institutions within capitalism. Hence, he concluded, there would be no socialist revolution.

I have no distinct memory, but I assume that when I got off the subway and back to my parents' home I reached for Emile Burns' *Handbook of Marxism* or some such source to find out why Burnham was wrong. The problem was I couldn't find an answer. Nor have I been able to find one during the more than half century since. In 1987 I rephrased Burnham's argument in *The Journal of American History*:

> The transition from capitalism to socialism presents problems
> that did not exist in the transition from feudalism to capitalism.
> In late medieval Europe, a discontented serf, a Protestant artisan,
> an experimental scientist, or an enterprising moneylender could
> do small-scale, piecemeal things to begin to build a new society

within the old. He could run away to a free city, print the Bible in the vernacular, drop stones from a leaning tower, or organize a corporation, all actions requiring few persons and modest amounts of capital, actions possible within the interstices of a decentralized feudal society. The twentieth-century variant of this process, in Third World countries, also permits revolutionary protagonists in guerrilla enclaves, like Yenan in China or the Sierra Maestra in Cuba, to build small-scale alternative societies, initiating land reform, health clinics, and literacy. But how can people take such meaningful small steps, begin such revolutionary reforms, in an interdependent society like that of the United States? A localized strategy runs into the problem of what might be called "socialism in one steel mill": the effort to do something qualitatively new, requiring tens of millions of dollars, in a hostile environment.

In the year 2002 one might rephrase the problem this way: if, as antiglobalization protesters affirm, another world is possible, how do we begin to build it, here and now?

I

Edward Thompson, too, was intensely concerned with the transition from capitalism to socialism, especially during the decade 1955–1965 in which he wrote and published *William Morris* and *The Making of the English Working Class*.

One of Thompson's first attempts to discuss the transition to socialism was an essay called "Socialist Humanism: An Epistle to the Philistines," published in 1957 in *The New Reasoner*.[2] There Thompson asserted that "mankind is caught up in the throes of a revolutionary transition to an entirely new form of society—a transition which must certainly reach its climax during this century." Several other comments about "the period of transition," "the phase of the transition," and "the transitional stage" are scattered throughout the essay. What is of greatest interest is Thompson's response to the thesis that the working class has not developed and cannot develop under capitalism a new society within the shell of the old. Here is what he wrote:

> The best, most fruitful ideas of Trotskyism—emphasis upon economic democracy and direct forms of political democracy—are expressed in fetishistic form: "workers' councils" and "Soviets" must be imposed as the only orthodoxy. But Britain teems with Soviets. We have a General Soviet of the T.U.C. [Trade Union

Congress] and trades soviets in every town: peace soviets and national soviets of women, elected parish, urban district and borough soviets.[3]

In these remarks, Thompson implicitly asks us to choose between two views of the transition from capitalism to socialism. One is expressed in the song by Wobbly Ralph Chaplin, "Solidarity Forever," when the song affirms: "We can bring to birth a new world from the ashes of the old." In this perspective the new world will arise, phoenixlike, after a great catastrophe or conflagration. The emergence of feudalism from pockets of local self-help after the collapse of the Roman Empire is presumably the exemplar of that kind of transition.

A second view of the transition from capitalism to socialism compares it to the transition from feudalism to capitalism. The Preamble to the IWW Constitution gives us a mantra for this perspective, declaring that "we are forming the structure of the new society within the shell of the old."

Thompson opted for the second paradigm. Confronting the question, Where is the proletarian new society within the shell of the old? Thompson answered as follows in another essay from the late 1950s, "Homage to Tom Maguire." There he discussed the genesis in the late nineteenth century of the Independent Labor Party, a party which—Thompson declared—"grew from the bottom up." According to Thompson:

> the ILP gave political expression to the various forms of independent or semi-independent working-class organisation which had been built and consolidated in the West Riding [of Yorkshire] in the previous thirty years [that is, from the 1860s to the 1890s]—co-operatives, trade unions, friendly societies, various forms of chapel or educational or economic "self-help."

This was a more concrete description of the "British soviets" invoked by Thompson in his essay on socialist humanism. Sheila Rowbotham remembers how, about this time, "Edward Thompson started to tell me about that northern [that is, north of Britain] socialism, how for a time preoccupation with changing all forms of human relationships had been central in a working-class movement."[4]

Edward Thompson's fullest engagement with the building of a working-class new society inside the shell of capitalism came in a book called *Out of Apathy*, published in 1960. Thompson wrote three essays for this volume. One is justly remembered and often reprinted: entitled "Outside the Whale," it is a tour de force in which Thompson details the retreat of Auden and Orwell from the enthusiasms of the 1930s. The other two essays, unjustly forgotten, are the introduction and conclusion to the volume.[5]

In these essays Thompson introduces a metaphor central to his view of the transition from capitalism to socialism: the rabbit warren. For a society to be crisscrossed by underground dens and passageways created by an oppositional class is, in Thompson's 1960s vocabulary, to be "warrened." British society, he wrote, "is warrened with democratic processes—committees, voluntary organisations, councils, electoral procedures." Because of the existence of such counterinstitutions, in Thompson's view a transition to socialism could develop from what was already in being, and from below. "Socialism, even at the point of revolutionary transition— perhaps at this point most of all—must grow from existing strengths. No one . . . can impose a socialist humanity from above."[6]

Thompson condemned the neglect of the issue of transition by persons calling themselves radicals. "[W]hat we mean to direct attention to is the extraordinary hiatus in contemporary labour thinking on this most crucial point of all—how, and by what means, is a transition to socialist society to take place." Further, in his view: "The absence of any theory of the transition to socialism is the consequence of capitulation to the conventions of capitalist politics."[7]

Here Thompson reaches a critical point in his argument. The difficulty in thinking about the transition from capitalism to socialism, he contends, derives in part from a mistaken notion about the difference between bourgeois and socialist revolutions to be found in the writings of . . . Joseph Stalin! Thompson finds the distinction most fully and dangerously expressed in Stalin's *On the Problems of Leninism* (1926). Here is what Thompson says in *Out of Apathy*:

> The conceptual barrier [to thinking about the transition from capitalism to socialism] derives . . . from a false distinction in Leninist doctrine between the bourgeois and the proletarian revolution. The bourgeois revolution (according to this legend) begins when "more or less finished forms of the capitalist order" already exist "within the womb of feudal society." Capitalism was able to grow up with feudalism, and to coexist with it—on uneasy terms—until prepared for the seizure of political power. But the proletarian revolution "begins when finished forms of the socialist order are either absent, or almost completely absent." Because it was supposed that forms of social ownership or democratic control over the means of production were incompatible with capitalist state power: "The bourgeois revolution is usually consummated with the seizure of power, whereas in the prole-

tarian revolution the seizure of power is only the beginning."

Thompson's footnote to this passage reads: "The quotations here are taken from Stalin's *On the Problems of Leninism* (1926); but the influence of this concept is to be found far outside the Communist tradition." I can confirm that the passages quoted by Thompson will be found on page 22 of volume 8 of the *Works* of Stalin (Moscow: Foreign Languages Publishing House, 1954).[8]

How does Thompson propose that we rebut the distinction between the bourgeois and proletarian revolutions? Thompson writes:

> [I]f we discard this dogma (the fundamentalist might meditate on the "interpenetration of opposites") we can read the evidence another way. It is not a case of either this or that. We must, at every point, see both—the surge forward and the containment, the public sector and its subordination to the private, the strength of trade unions and their parasitism upon capitalist growth, the welfare services and their poor-relation status. The countervailing powers are there, and the equilibrium (which is an equilibrium within capitalism) is precarious. It could be tipped back towards authoritarianism. But it could also be heaved forward, by popular pressures of great intensity, to the point where the powers of democracy cease to be countervailing and become the active dynamic of society in their own right. This is revolution.[9]

Thompson is thinking dialectically. X need not be A or non-A. X can be both A and B, depending on the context, because both the context and X itself are constantly changing.

I cannot resist further quotation from these most politically important of all the words Edward Thompson ever wrote.

> Certainly, the transition can be defined, in the widest historical sense, as a transfer of class power: the dislodgment of the power of capital from the "commanding heights" and the assertion of the power of socialist democracy. This is the historical watershed between "last stage" capitalism and dynamic socialism— the point at which the socialist potential is liberated, the public sector assumes the dominant role, subordinating the private to its command, and over a very great area of life the priorities of need override those of profit. But this point cannot be defined in narrow political (least of all parliamentary) terms; nor can we be certain, in advance, in what context the breakthrough will be made. What is more important to insist upon is that it is neces-

sary to find out the breaking point, not by theoretical specula-
tion alone, but in practice by unrelenting reforming pressure in
many fields, which are designed to reach a revolutionary culmi-
nation. And this will entail a confrontation, throughout society,
between two systems, two ways of life.[10]

Throughout the emphasis is on the positive, building on existing
strengths, as opposed to a scenario of catastrophe and apocalypse. In
Thompson's words:

> [S]uch a revolution demands the maximum enlargement of
> positive demands, the deployment of constructive skills with-
> in a conscious revolutionary strategy—or, in William Morris'
> words, the "making of Socialists." . . . Alongside the industrial
> workers, we should see the teachers who want better schools,
> scientists who wish to advance research, welfare workers who
> want hospitals, actors who want a National Theatre, technicians
> impatient to improve industrial organisation. Such people do
> not want these things only and always, any more than all indus-
> trial workers are always "class conscious" and loyal to their great
> community values. But these affirmatives coexist, fitfully and
> incompletely, with the ethos of the Opportunity State. It is the
> business of socialists to draw the line, not between a staunch
> but diminishing minority and an unredeemable majority, but
> between the monopolists and the people—to foster the "societal
> instincts" and inhibit the acquisitive. Upon these positives, and
> not upon the débris of a smashed society, the socialist commu-
> nity must be built.[11]

Edward Thompson touched upon these same themes five years later,
in the course of his polemic with Perry Anderson and Tom Nairn entitled "The Peculiarities of the English." The occasion was the comment
of Anderson and Nairn that after Chartism, which crested about 1850,
the English working class ceased to be a revolutionary force. Note once
again the dialectical caste of Thompson's response as well as the recur-
rent comparison of working-class institutions to a "warren."

> [T]he workers, having failed to overthrow capitalist society, pro-
> ceeded to warren it from end to end. This "caesura" [after 1850] is
> exactly the period in which the characteristic class institutions of
> the Labour movement were built up—trade unions, trade coun-
> cils, T.U.C., co-ops, and the rest—which have endured to this day.
> It was part of the logic of this new direction that each advance

within the framework of capitalism simultaneously involved the working class more deeply in the status quo. As they improved their position by organization within the workshop, so they became more reluctant to engage in quixotic outbreaks which might jeopardize gains accumulated at such cost. Each assertion of working-class influence within the bourgeois-democratic state machinery, simultaneously involved them as partners (even if antagonistic partners) in the running of the machine. . . .

We need not necessarily agree with Wright Mills that this indicates that the working class can be a revolutionary class only in its formative years; but we must, I think, recognize that once a certain climactic moment is passed, the opportunity for a certain *kind* of revolutionary movement passes irrevocably. . . .

[I]t is possible to envisage three kinds of socialist transition, none of which have in fact ever been successfully carried through. First, the syndicalist revolution in which the class institutions displace the existing State machine; I suspect that the moment for such a revolution, if it was ever practicable, has passed in the West. Second, through a more or less constitutional political party, based on the political institutions, with a very clearly articulated socialist strategy, whose cumulative reforms bring the country to a critical point of class equilibrium, from which a rapid revolutionary transition is pressed through. [Attentive Thompson watchers will recognize this second scenario as that set forth five years before in *Out of Apathy*.] Third, through further far-reaching changes in the sociological composition of the groups which entail the break-up of the old class institutions and value system, and the creation of new ones.[12]

Writing in 1965, Edward thought that some combination of the second and third strategies might hold most promise. The bottom line for all discussion, in his view, was: "It is abundantly evident that working people have, within capitalist society, thrown up positions of 'countervailing power.'" The New Left—already in 1965 he calls it "the former New Left"—had sought to pursue "reformist tactics within a revolutionary strategy." But whatever the verbal trappings, he concluded:

[W]e have stated a problem, but are no nearer its solution. The real work of analysis remains: the sociological analysis of changing groups within the wage-earning and salaried strata; the points of potential antagonism and alliance; the economic analysis, the cultural analysis, the political analysis, not only of forms of State power, but also of the bureaucracies of the Labour Movement.[13]

Edward Thompson did not himself pursue the analysis for which he called. In 1965, the same year in which "The Peculiarities of the English" was published, he took a full-time position at Warwick University and disappeared in the general direction of the eighteenth century. Much that was marvelous ensued, and in the early 1980s Thompson emerged from intellectual work to spend half a dozen years in ceaseless agitation against the nuclear arms race, an agitation that may have hastened his premature death. My point is only that, to the best of my knowledge, he did not pursue further what he had termed the unresolved problem of the transition from capitalism to socialism. We shall have to attempt that task ourselves.

II

If another world is possible, and we want to build it within the womb or shell of capitalist society, how should we proceed? What institutions can serve the working class in "warrening" (Edward Thompson's phrase) the old society with the emerging institutions of the new?

The most obvious answer is trade unions. In "Value, Price and Profit," Karl Marx wrote in 1865: "Trades Unions work well as centres of resistance against the encroachments of capital." The next year, in instructions drafted for the British delegation to the 1866 congress of the First International, Marx expressly compared the work of trade unions as "centres of organization of the working class" to what "the medieval municipalities and communes did for the middle class."

However, the limitations of trade unions soon became apparent. Capitalism was furthest advanced in Great Britain. In their *History of Trade Unionism*, published in 1894, and *Industrial Democracy*, published in 1898, Sidney and Beatrice Webb summed up the evolution of trade unions in that country. The Webbs found that the "revolutionary period" in the history of the British labor movement was at the beginning, in 1829–1842, and that the business unionism of the British labor movement at the close of the nineteenth century was good, or at any rate "inevitable."

The Webbs' conclusions powerfully influenced Lenin, who together with his wife Krupskaya translated the Webbs' *Industrial Democracy* while in Siberian exile. In *What Is to Be Done?*, published in 1902, Lenin proposed a revolutionary strategy that accepted the findings of the Webbs with regard to the development of trade unions. "The history of all countries," he wrote, "shows that the working class, exclusively by its own effort, is able to develop only trade-union consciousness." Socialist consciousness could only be brought to workers "from without." The spontaneous labor movement, Lenin wrote elsewhere in the same pamphlet, "is pure and simple trade unionism." Hence the task of socialists was "to *divert* the labour movement, with its spontaneous trade-unionist striving," and bring it under the wing of revolutionary Social Democracy.

Only three years later—dialectically, as it were—the Russian revolution of 1905 imposed a powerful corrective to Lenin's analysis in *What Is to Be Done?* Without significant assistance from middle-class revolutionaries or from the various revolutionary parties, the Russian working class embarked on a yearlong general strike and created autonomous institutions from below: the improvised central labor bodies known as "soviets." Throughout this course of self-activity, workers sacrificed and died for political objectives as well as economic ones. Rosa Luxemburg found in the revolution of 1905 a dramatic refutation of what she termed Lenin's "pitiless centralism," which, in her view, imposed a "blind subordination" of all party organs to the party center and expressed "the sterile spirit of the overseer."

There the debate has rested ever since.

Howard Zinn

It would be comical for me to pretend to what is generally understood as "objectivity" in discussing the work of Howard Zinn. Howard was one of my closest friends. My copy of the Twentieth Anniversary Edition of *A People's History of the United States* is inscribed: "For Staughton and Alice, good, good friends, with admiration and love. Howie."

Howard Zinn recruited me for the history department of Spelman College, a college in Atlanta for African American women, in December 1960. Our two families spent time together in New Hampshire during the summer of 1961. One day Howard, his children Myla and Jeff, and I climbed a mountain together. (Historical note: He says in his autobiography that it was Mt. Monadnock. It was Mt. Chocorua.) Howard comments on the fact that I "came from a background completely different" from his own. Yet as our mountain-climbing conversation that day "went back and forth on every political issue under the sun—race, class, war, violence, nationalism, justice, fascism, capitalism, socialism, and more—it was clear that our social philosophies, our values, were extraordinarily similar."[1]

But I would protest any assertion that because we were close friends and looked at the world in similar ways, I am disqualified from offering incisive commentary on Howard's work. Any such argument would make the error of assuming that in order to be unbiased a historian must not have taken part in the events described, or that the greater the historian's distance from the object of study, the more valuable his commentary is likely to be. This logic would hold that Thucydides should not have analyzed the wars of Athens, or Trotsky the history of the Russian Revolution. It should be obvious that while familiarity heightens the danger of bias, it also makes possible knowledge of facts that the detached academic has no way of knowing.

The Ex-Bombardier

The Howard Zinn who chronicled SNCC's striving to overcome racism, who then wrote *A People's History* and shepherded it through later editions, was a steadfast advocate for an unchanging point of view.

But one aspect of Howard's life exhibited an equally dramatic reversal of perspectives. During World War II, Howard was so eager to get into combat that he gave up a shipyard job that would have kept him safe for the duration of the war, and arranged with his draft board to "volunteer for induction," even obtaining permission to mail his induction notice to himself. During flight training he was similarly anxious to get to Europe, and twice he "traded with other bombardiers to get on the short list for overseas."[2]

The eager bombardier of World War II became a passionate opponent of all conceivable modern wars and the governments that lie about them. How did this change happen? What does it mean? And is it possible that Howard Zinn will be remembered most of all as an opponent of war? Howard tells us in his autobiography how and why his outlook began to change during World War II.

Howard had made friends with a gunner in another crew, who, like himself, read books and was interested in politics. One day his friend said, "You know, this is not a war against fascism. It's an imperialist war."

Startled, Howard responded, "Then why are you here?"

His friend replied, "To talk to guys like you." Two weeks later his friend's plane was shot down and the whole crew killed.[3]

Then when the war was almost over, the briefing officer said that they were going to bomb a French town named Royan. A few thousand German soldiers had retreated to Royan. They weren't fighting, just waiting for the war to end. The planes in Howard's squadron were not going to carry their usual load but, instead, thirty one-hundred-pound canisters of "jellied gasoline." The town of Royan was decimated, the many victims French as well as German. Only long after the war did Howard recognize that this was an early use of napalm.[4]

At the time of his discharge, Howard spontaneously wrote on the folder in which he kept papers concerning his military service, "Never again."[5] But exactly what this meant for him evolved over the years.

At the time I came to know Howard in Atlanta in the early 1960s, he was extremely fond of Joseph Heller's novel *Catch-22*. Therein Yossarian, an Air Force bombardier (as Howard had been), says, "The enemy is anybody who's going to get you killed, no matter which side he's on." In fall 1962, when the mayor of Atlanta wired President Kennedy that Atlantans supported as one man the president's threat to go to war over missiles in Cuba, Howard, along with the staff of the nearby SNCC headquarters and a number of teachers, myself included, picketed in protest. And it is too often forgotten today that SNCC took a position in support of men who refused service in Vietnam a year before SDS did so.

Howard's opinions on war and nonviolence are scattered in short essays through a number of books. Annoyingly, in some of these books the essays are not dated, and it is difficult to follow the development of Howard's ideas. I have selected a few of these short writings that I believe to be representative, first of Howard's attitude toward pacifism, then of his increasing commitment to nonviolence.

"The Force of Nonviolence" was written in 1962 and published in *The Nation*.[6] Therein Howard heaped praise on the possibilities of nonviolence but rejected the "absolutism" of pacifists. Within SNCC, that part of the civil rights movement with which Howard most identified, the attitude toward violence varied from person to person and overall was conflicted and ambivalent. As Howard puts it in this early essay, the theories of those who engaged in the desegregation struggle were "less developed than their actions." Indeed, he wrote, the theory of "the nonviolence people" was "muddy."

It seemed to Howard at that time that "people know, deep inside, even if they can't articulate the reasons, that there are times when violence is justified." Nonviolence "seen as absolute pacifism" is only one of two linked values that "humanitarian people share—peace and social justice."

> The nonviolent absolutist, in all logic, may have to forego social change, putting himself in the contradictory position of maintaining a status quo that tolerates violence like capital punishment and police brutality against Negroes. On the other hand, people who are prepared to pursue any course of action leading to social change may find themselves in the contradictory position of using such violent and uncontrollable means that there is no society left to enjoy the benefits of the changes they seek.

Accordingly, one must "weigh, weigh, weigh" one set of desirable values against another. On the whole, "nonviolent techniques . . . seem the only sensible answer to a world sitting in a mine field and yet needing to move."

In an undated essay titled "Pacifism and War," Howard remarked again: "I have never used the word 'pacifist' to describe myself, because it suggests something absolute, and I am suspicious of absolutes."[7]

Thus Howard's early perspective concerning violence and nonviolence expressed great support for nonviolence but made room for particular circumstances when violence might be unavoidable. Action was more important than words. Howard quoted Albert Einstein: "Wars will stop when men refuse to fight."[8] Yet his overall position was like that of Archbishop Oscar Romero of El Salvador, who condemned "institutional violence," "terrorism," and violence disproportionate to the aggression prompting its use, but said that there were some situations when violence was legitimate.

One early influence to which Howard referred repeatedly was a book titled *Johnny Got His Gun* by an author named Dalton Trumbo. Howard called it "perhaps the most disturbing anti-war novel ever written." It tells of a young man who became a soldier and not only lost his four limbs but became a slab of flesh with "no face, blind, deaf, unable to speak," yet still alive. During my last telephone call with Howard, he commented bitterly on the fact that after Germany invaded the Soviet Union, the Communist Party of the United States (and perhaps Trumbo himself) prevented the reissuance of this novel lest it detract from the war effort in which the Soviet Union was involved.

Howard Zinn's last public speech was titled "Three Holy Wars." It was delivered at Boston University on November 11 (the day that in my childhood we called Armistice Day), 2009. The three "holy wars" were the American Revolution, the Civil War, and World War II.

Howard asked whether the American Revolution was necessary. "How about Canada? . . . They are independent of England. They did not fight a bloody war. It took longer. Sometimes it takes longer if you don't want to kill."

A kind of electric shock went through me as I read those words. I recalled how in the 1960s Howard had been so careful to distinguish his views from the "absolutism" of pacifists. He seemed to be espousing in the last weeks of his life a sort of de facto pacifism, a position that amounted to pacifism even if you used different words.

Proceeding to the Civil War, Howard asked essentially the same thing. Yes, slavery had been abolished, but did that require the deaths of 600,000 Union and Confederate soldiers? (Since Howard's death, a new survey counted the number of "missing males" in census data and raised the estimated number of Civil War fatalities to 750,000.) Elsewhere in the Western Hemisphere, Howard insisted, slavery had been abolished without a bloody civil war.

He went on to his own war, World War II. Howard's essential message was that when you bomb from thirty thousand feet, this is modern warfare, you do things from a distance, it's very impersonal. You just press a button and somebody dies. You don't see them. . . . I didn't see any human beings. I didn't see what was happening below. I didn't see children screaming, I didn't see arms about ripped off people. No. You just drop bombs. You see little flashes of light down below as the bombs hit. That's it. And you don't think.[9]

Was this history? Repentance? Prophetic denunciation? All of the foregoing? Howard's history of saturation bombing by Allied bombers, from within the event, is indeed history from below (as well as from high above). Perhaps he exemplified thereby something just as powerful and memorable as anything he could write about persons he had never known, like Christopher Columbus.

Howard Zinn was an early prototype of today's typical conscientious objector: a man or woman who volunteers for military service, finds it impossible to take part in conduct perceived to be "war crimes," yet remains uncertain how he or she would respond if the United States were attacked. It is hypocritical that the United States government recognizes as conscientious objectors only members of fringe Protestant sects (like the Quakers, to which I belong) who oppose "war in any form" on the basis of "religious training and belief." After World War II the United States executed certain German and Japanese defendants who, a tribunal concluded, had committed war crimes in that particular war, World War II. Must we then not recognize as bona fide conscientious objectors soldiers who refuse to continue criminal conduct in a particular war, or who, having taken part in such conduct, like Howard Zinn declare "Never again"?

Overcoming Racism

Howard Zinn and I were colleagues at Spelman College in the academic years 1961–1962 and 1962–1963. Our families lived on campus, around the corner from each other in the same building.

It strikes me as strange that so-called whiteness theory, while no doubt a form of history from the bottom up, seems wholly preoccupied with why some white workers become racists and devotes almost no attention to how racism can be overcome. It was otherwise in Atlanta in the early 1960s. During those years the inevitable subject of conversation was how a society so saturated with racism as the southern United States might free itself from that miasma. The Spelman College campus was roiled by conflict arising when the young ladies enrolled there went downtown to picket local restaurants and department stores, to sit in the "whites only" gallery at the state legislature, or to attempt to use segregated public libraries.

In a typical incident illustrative of the crisis atmosphere, I was awakened one night by a phone call to the effect that a friend who taught at Atlanta University, his wife, and their two young daughters had all been arrested while peacefully picketing. Morris and Fannie were in the city jail downtown. Would I go to the juvenile detention facility on the city outskirts and bail out the two girls? (This is only the beginning of the story.)

Howard explored the American dilemma of racism in a book largely forgotten today, *The Southern Mystique*. The book's central argument is made clear in a journal Howard kept (now in the Zinn Papers at New York University) while drafting this book. He was simultaneously beginning to do oral histories for his next book, *SNCC: The New Abolitionists*. Thus an entry on January 10, 1963, reports: "Ran into Ruby Doris Smith—she finishes school this semester, will do field work for SNCC thereafter. Told her want to tape her experiences."

On that same date Howard described a town hall meeting in which he took part together with Eugene Patterson, editor of the leading Atlanta newspaper; Macon mayor Ed Wilson; and Sam Williams, a black professor. "Both Sam and Patterson said at different points that [we] must change Southern white behavior before [we can] change his mind—squares exactly with what I've been writing about."

The next day, January 11, the journal reports the visit of a Princeton sociologist named Berger. On January 19, after interviewing Julian Bond at the Zinns' apartment and engaging in "concentrated talk with Negroes in all sorts of situations," Professor Berger "came over for a last chat before departure." Howard and his guest "disputed a little about the future," Howard records.

> He sees, after legal desegregation, a plateau, no real improvement, with whites continu[ing] to be prejudiced and no indication of change. . . . My argument: Yes, it seems strong, and it is at the moment, but it can change quickly—with contact. When housing and jobs become open, when white salesmen begin to have lunch— thru business necessity—with Negroes and stay at the same hotel with them, and so on—I cited my warehouse experience.

What did Howard mean by his "warehouse experience"? After classes at NYU and Columbia, Howard worked from four in the afternoon to midnight in a warehouse loading eighty-pound containers onto trailer trucks. In his autobiography, Howard explains the relevance of this experience to the theme of his conversation with Professor Berger. The warehouse crew included, along with several whites, a black man and a Honduran immigrant.[10]

In Howard's view, "equal-status contact" over a period of time, as among members of the warehouse crew, was what would cause racial attitudes to change. *The Southern Mystique* presents a sophisticated rationale for this approach. Persons inclined to dismiss Howard Zinn as a shallow popularizer should take a look at the "bibliographical notes" to his book. Here one finds works of history, like Stanley Elkins's *Slavery*; *The Strange Career of Jim Crow* by C. Vann Woodward; W. E. B. DuBois's *The Souls of Black Folk*; *From Slavery to Freedom* by John Hope Franklin; and W. J. Cash, *The Mind of the South*. Howard also cites sociologists Ross, Cooley, Mannheim, Merton, and Franklin Frazier, and psychologists Harry Stack Sullivan, Kurt Lewin, and Gardner Murphy.

Howard's logic goes as follows. Everyone has a hierarchy of values. For many persons, racism may be one such value, but it is unlikely to be the thing that anyone cares about most. Change the external requirements of daily life so that whites must engage in equal-status contact with blacks in order to achieve their highest priorities, and over time racist attitudes will change in response.

In his autobiography Howard tells us how this idea first occurred to him. After he joined the Air Force and finished training, Howard found himself on a luxury liner headed for Europe. There were sixteen thousand troops on board. The four thousand who were black "slept in the depths of the ship near the engine room" and ate last, in, so he comments in *A People's History*, "a bizarre reminder of the slave voyages of old."

On the fifth day at sea there was a mix-up. The last shift poured into the dining room before the previous shift had finished eating, filling in wherever white men had left. A white sergeant sitting next to a black man called out to Howard (who was by then a lieutenant), "Get him out of here until I finish." Howard refused, and the sergeant, apparently caring more about his food than about who sat next to him, finished his meal.[11]

Howard's entry for March 3, 1963, offers the journal's most extended explanation of this strategy for overcoming racism. The YWCA had brought eighty Negro and white college students from all over the South to a conference in Gatlinburg, Tennessee. Howard was invited as a presenter. Regardless of "all the nonsense associated with Y conferences," he commented in his journal, it was a "revolutionary act, really a marvelous thing to see. . . . Two days of living together are worth two decades of reading or talking about 'good race relations.'" The young women didn't need to "talk about these things, just live them."

My own experience with equal-status interracial contact among workers and prisoners strongly corroborates Howard Zinn's conclusion. Briefly, here are the stories of two white men who changed what they thought about blacks after a period of equal-status contact.

George Sullivan grew up in southern Illinois, a community awash with racial prejudice. (David Roediger grew up in the same setting and describes it in the opening pages of his *Wages of Whiteness*.) As a young adult George joined the Air Force. He was moved to a new base at about the same time that President Truman's executive order desegregating the military came into effect. George found himself in a barracks where everyone but himself was African American.

After several days of uncomfortable silence, there came a time when George was sitting on the steps of the barracks with orders to sew on his sergeant stripes by the next day or lose that promotion. But he couldn't sew on the stripes because, working as a meat cutter, he had cut three or four of his fingers.

> I was sitting there by myself just wondering what to do. One of the guys in the barracks . . . came out and said, "Have you already got your stripes?" I said, "Yeah, I bought them already." He said, "Well if you go get them I'll sew them on for you." So that was the first thing that really broke the ice. He sat and sewed those stripes on my uniform while we got to know each other.[12]

Prisoners, too, experience equal-status contact. The most dramatic example I know of the effect of equal-status contact on prisoners' attitudes was set forth in a long letter to me by a young white man from South Carolina. He had come to the Ohio State Penitentiary as "a stone cold racist." But "three years at O.S.P. has changed that 100%. It's the WHITE police, administrators, and nurses who treat me like a 'nigger'; treat all of us like that."

This young man had been watching public television. "I used to be proud of white historical domination," he explains,

> the way whites just crushed and conquered all who stood in their path historically. But now when I watch documentaries on PBS like "Conquistadors" or "The West" it makes me mad because in those conquests and legal genocides I now see the arrogance of Lt. ____ or the administrators at O.S.P., with the blind assumption of superiority by all the frontiersmen/conquistadors/correctional officers. . . . It makes me respect the Indians who fought to the death . . . or the Incan/Aztec natives who stood up to the

conquistadors . . . or the slaves who found the courage to revolt.

Thus, fifty years after the publication of *The Southern Mystique*, I find that my own experience tends to support the strategy for overcoming racism that it sets forth.

A People's History

Howard is, of course, best known to the world as the author of *A People's History of the United States.*

This book was first published in 1980, roughly fifteen years after *The Southern Mystique* and *SNCC*, and thirty years before Howard's death. As of this writing (summer 2013), something like two million copies have been sold. The book has been internationally recognized, as by the Goncourt Prize in France. The governor of Indiana has sought to ban *A People's History* from Indiana public schools.

According to Robert Cohen, who is working with correspondence in the Zinn archives, the great majority of the (generally enthusiastic) letters from students across the country concern the book's first chapter, about Columbus. I have a personal reason for appreciating that chapter's critique of Harvard professor Samuel Eliot Morison. Morison was a biographer of Columbus who, according to *A People's History*, mentions genocide in passing but waxes enthusiastic about Columbus's seamanship. I took a course with Professor Morison as a Harvard undergraduate and remember him lecturing—in his yachting whites!

So how shall we evaluate the historical phenomenon of *A People's History*? No doubt it is too soon to make a final judgment. I shall offer a preliminary assessment.

First I shall present a critique of "people's history." Then I shall attempt to say what Howard would say—indeed, has said—in response. My conclusion is that if we listen carefully to Howard's description of his intentions, many criticisms fade into irrelevance.

A Critique of People's History

Howard Zinn's *People's History* is not the first panoramic history of the United States from a Left point of view. I have a mental image of myself in the high school library, enthralled by *The Rise of American Civilization* by Charles and Mary Beard. Perhaps its most distinctive argument was that the Civil War was a second American Revolution. Later Leo Huberman, labor educator and coeditor of *Monthly Review*, published a shorter survey history titled *We, the People*.

Nor is Howard Zinn's the first "people's history" of the United States. Several years before Howard published *A People's History*, a young man named Harvey Wasserman sent him *Harvey Wasserman's History of the United States*, published by Harper and Row in 1972. At Harvey's request Howard wrote the introduction, specifically identifying the book as a "people's history."

I believe that one reason "people's history" was attractive to Howard, as it was to other progressive historians, was the political atmosphere on the Left during the years in which he came to adulthood. The idea of a united, radical American people was abroad in the land in the late 1930s. The Communist Party was by far the largest and most influential radical group in the United States at the time. Beginning in 1935, the worldwide Communist movement sought to create coalitions of all groups and persons who might be enlisted to resist fascist aggression. The strategy promoted by the Party was known as "the Popular Front."[13]

In his autobiography Howard provides a sketch of his interest in world politics as an adolescent.[14] He was "reading books about fascism in Europe." He was fascinated by a book about Mussolini's seizure of power in Italy and could not get out of his mind "the courage of the Socialist deputy Matteoti," who was dragged from his home and murdered by fascist thugs. *The Brown Book of the Nazi Terror* described what was happening in Hitler's Germany. And "the Nazi war machine" was beginning to expand westward and eastward.

The Spanish Civil War was "the event closest to all of us," Howard writes, because American radicals were crossing the Atlantic to fight with the international brigades against Franco. Howard knew a few such young men personally. So did I. In May 1936, an Ohioan named Sam Levinger carried me on his shoulders in a gigantic May Day parade in New York City. In September 1937, Sam was fatally wounded in the battle of Belchite.[15]

The Popular Front political strategy had repercussions for the writing of history. The idea of a "people" united for democracy and against fascism was central. There was talk of the democratic tradition of Jefferson, Jackson, and Lincoln. There was even talk of Communism as "twentieth-century Americanism." I was half a dozen years younger than Howard but vividly remember folk dancing at the hall of the furriers' union and learning the songs of anti-Franco combatants in the Spanish Civil War.

The intellectual atmosphere associated with Popular Front politics and focused on "the people" extended far beyond Communists and their supporters. Carl Sandburg wrote an iconic poem called "The People, Yes," as well as a multivolume biography of Lincoln. During World

War II it was natural that concepts of a united "people" came to the fore. Even after the war, Arthur Schlesinger Jr., well-known for his anti-Communism, wrote a paean to "Jacksonian Democracy" that today seems to ignore the displacement of the Cherokees much as Samuel Eliot Morison failed to focus on the destruction of the Arawak Indians who had greeted Columbus.

Howard's history of "the people" at first glance seems vulnerable to the criticism that what he calls "the people" has never really existed. That criticism of the idea of "the people" was memorably expressed by the late Edmund S. Morgan, writing about an earlier historical period in a book called *Inventing the People*:

> Government requires make-believe. Make believe that the King is divine, make believe that he can do no wrong or make believe that the voice of the people is the voice of God. Make believe that the people have a voice or make believe that the representatives of the people are the people. . . .
>
> The people . . . are never visible as such. Before we ascribe sovereignty to the people we have to imagine that there is such a thing, something that we personify as though it were a single body, capable of thinking, of acting, of making decisions and carrying them out, something quite apart from government, superior to government, and able to alter or remove a government at will, a collective entity more powerful and less fallible than a king or than any individual within it or than any group of individuals it singles out to govern it.
>
> To sustain a fiction so palpably contrary to fact is not easy.[16]

I believe Howard conceded that he sought to find in the past examples of heroism and persistence among ordinary people that might encourage us today. That effort is self-evidently vulnerable to the doctrine that historians should seek to discover what happened, not to create a "usable past" with imagined relevance to the present. How would Howard answer that charge? How did he answer it?

Howard's Response

A good place to begin Howard's response to critiques like that of Edmund Morgan is his introduction to Harvey Wasserman's book, which began: "Why should we read *Harvey Wasserman's History of the United States* when we can read a regular and respectable textbook written by some regular and respectable historian? Because his book is a beautiful example of people's history."[17]

Howard then went on to ask, "What is 'people's history,' and why do we need it?" He cited earlier texts that pointed to that perspective: Harold Laswell's definition of politics as "who gets what, how, and why?" and Charles Beard's *Economic Interpretation of the Constitution of the United States.*

We seem to think, Howard continued, that a book is unbiased if it repeats the bias of all the books that went before it. In reality, every history book has a point of view, every historian is subjective.

Then comes a crucial paragraph. After reciting the misdeeds of a series of greedy corporate executives, Howard says of their continuing impact on events:

> To know that this has been true for a long time, that it is a persistent fact of American history, is important. It means these conditions do not belong to one period of the past. *Here we find a use in history.* If it shows conditions as continuous and deep-rooted—in this case, the power of corporate wealth behind politics, behind everyday life—it suggests to us that more radical measures than electing another president or passing another program in Congress will be necessary to change these conditions. It suggests that we will have to dig to the roots—to change our thinking, our relations with one another, to transform our institutions, our economic system, our day-to-day existence.[18]

Note that in his autobiography, published fourteen years after *A People's History*, Howard uses almost identical words to describe how he became a radical after he was beaten by police in Times Square. "From that moment on," he says, "I was a radical. . . . The situation required not just a new president or new laws, but an uprooting of the old order, the introduction of a new kind of society—cooperative, peaceful, egalitarian."[19]

In the Wasserman introduction, Howard moves on to the affirmation that in order for the American people to "trust in themselves," they "need to know something which history knows": that people "apparently without power themselves can create power by determining not to be controlled, by acting with others to change their lives." History "should not leave us with a dark and hopeless vision." It should leave us, as does Wasserman's book, with "the good feeling of standing alongside people who fought back."

In a book called *The Politics of History*, written at about the same time as his introduction to Wasserman's history, Howard reiterated his ideas with reference to his master's essay on the Ludlow Massacre of 1914. The massacre came to his attention, Howard says, "first in a song by Woody Guthrie . . . then in a chapter of the book by Samuel Yellen, *American Labor Struggles*, written in 1936." It was a dreadful event, in which National Guardsmen acting on behalf of Rockefeller interests fired into tents in which striking miners, their wives, and their children had taken refuge, and then set them on fire. According to Howard, eleven people were killed by gunfire, and thirteen more (eleven children and two women) when the Guardsmen set fire to the tents.

Howard's essay on Ludlow makes clear that he was able to write detailed narrative history based on fully cited primary sources. But the detailed rendering of a particular past event did not satisfy Howard. He makes this clear at the end of his Ludlow essay, reprinted in *The Politics of History*. There he writes:

> How shall we read the story of the Ludlow massacre? As another "interesting" event of the past? Or as supporting evidence for an analysis of that long present which spans 1914 and 1970 [the year in which he was writing]? If it is read narrowly, as an incident in the history of the trade union movement and the coal industry, then it is an angry splotch in the past, fading rapidly amidst new events. If it is read as a commentary on a larger question—the relationship of government to corporate power and of both to movements of social protest—then we are dealing with the present.[20]

In other words, Howard wanted history to be a set of generalizations formed by connecting the stories of comparable historical events occurring at different points in time.

Is this an effort to create a "usable past"? The answer is yes. But all history seeks to make some use of the past. And Howard Zinn is not distorting past events, except in a sense that is true of every historical undertaking: he selects some facts for emphasis and gives less attention to others. He selects stories showing the ruthlessness of corporate power and the unappreciated resilience and fortitude of poor and oppressed people.

And that is exactly what he says again in the last chapter and afterword of *A People's History*. He is not describing a past event or making a prediction but expressing a hope. Using the mantra later popularized by the Occupy movement, Howard incisively contrasts the 99 percent with the well-to-do 1 percent. He says that he is "taking the liberty of uniting those 99 percent as 'the people,'" writing a history "that attempts to represent their submerged, deflected, common interest."[21] By uniting them as characters in a single historical narrative he seeks to unite them in fact, as a real force in making history. He wonders how the foreign policies of the United States would look if we wiped out the national boundaries of the world, at least in our minds, and thought of all children everywhere as our own. Then we could never drop an atomic bomb on Hiroshima, or napalm in Vietnam, or wage war anywhere, because wars, especially in our time, are always wars against children, indeed our children.[22]

Working-Class Self-Activity

As in the title of his best-known book, Howard Zinn often invoked "the people." But the core of Howard's personal experience of the power of the people was a series of immersions in specifically working-class collective action. I believe that a lifelong commitment to working- class self-activity is at the heart of Howard Zinn's radicalism. In contrast to the diffuse mutual aid of "the people" or temporary coalitions of soldiers and prisoners against repression, the solidarity of persons who work together remains the core of resistance to capitalism and prefigures a better society. Incidentally, working-class solidarity offers a link between the discussion in Part I of this little book and the material in Part II.

One can follow this thread from beginning to end of Howard's experience. Hard labor as an apprentice shipfitter for three years during World War II was Howard's "introduction to the world of heavy industry," he tells us in his autobiography. "What made the job bearable was the steady pay and the accompanying dignity of being a workingman, like my father." But "most important" for Howard was that he found among his workmates "a small group of friends, fellow apprentices—some of them shipfitters like myself, others shipwrights, machinists, pipefitters, sheetmetal workers—who were young radicals, determined to do something to change the world."

What they decided to do, since they were excluded from the craft unions of the skilled workers, was "to organize the apprentices into a union, an association." Three hundred young workers joined. Howard says that this was his "introduction to actual participation in a labor movement." He and his coworkers, Howard writes, were doing "what working people had done through the centuries, creating little spaces of culture and friendship to make up for the dreariness of the work itself."

Howard and three others were elected to be officers of the apprentices' association. "We met one evening a week to read books on politics and economics and socialism, and talk about world affairs."[23]

After his service in the Air Force, Howard shared the following experience with the other truck-loaders at the warehouse.

We were all members of the union (District 65), which had a reputation of being "left-wing." But we, the truck-loaders, were more left than the union, which seemed hesitant to interfere with the loading operation of this warehouse.

We were angry about our working conditions, having to load outside on the sidewalk in bad weather with no rain or snow gear available to us. We kept asking the company for gear, with no results. One night, late, the rain began pelting down. We stopped work, said we would not continue unless we had a binding promise of rain gear.

The supervisor was beside himself. That truck had to get out that night to meet the schedule, he told us. He had no authority to promise anything. We said, "Tough shit. We're not getting drenched for the damn schedule." He got on the phone, nervously calling a company executive at his home, interrupting a dinner party. He came back from the phone. "Okay, you'll get your gear." The next workday we arrived at the warehouse and found a line of shiny new raincoats and rainhats.[24]

These personal experiences stood by Howard when, in *A People's History*, he came to the worker self-activity of the 1930s. Howard did not agree with typical liberal and radical celebration of the creation of the CIO by John L. Lewis. He insists that "it was rank-and-file insurgencies that pushed the union leadership, AFL and CIO, into action." He offers a detailed and affectionate description of the first sit-down strikes and how the tactic spread. Then he writes:

The sit-downs were especially dangerous to the system because they were not controlled by the regular union leadership. . . . Unions were not wanted by employers, but they were more controllable—more stabilizing for the system than the wildcat strikes, the factory occupations of the rank and file. In the spring of 1937, a New York Times article carried the headline "Unauthorized Sit-Downs Fought by CIO Unions." The story read: "Strict orders have been issued to all organizers and representatives that they will be dismissed if they authorize any stoppages of work without the consent of the international officers. . . ." The Times quoted John L. Lewis, dynamic leader of the CIO: "A CIO contract is adequate protection against sit-downs, lie-downs, or any other kind of strike."

Howard goes on to observe that the Communist Party, in its anxiety to create the widest possible coalition against fascism, "seemed to take the same position."[25]

Summing up, Howard described the National Labor Relations Act and the structure and practice of the new CIO trade unions as "two sophisticated ways of controlling direct labor action." The CIO might be "a militant and aggressive union," yet it would "channel the workers' insurrectionary energy into contracts, negotiations, union meetings, and try to minimize strikes, in order to build large, influential, even respectable organizations." Accordingly, Howard concluded that the history of the 1930s seemed to support the analysis of Richard Cloward and Frances Fox Piven, who argued in their book *Poor People's Movements* "that labor won most during its spontaneous uprisings, before the unions were recognized or well organized."[26]

Once again as a professor at Boston University, Howard confronted personally issues arising from the efforts of workers to organize themselves. To begin with, teachers like Howard pursued the right to organize. In addition, responding to the arrogant administration of President John Silber, workers of all kinds, such as clerical workers, librarians, and staff at the nursing school, also insisted on their rights under the National Labor Relations Act. Howard consistently advocated not only aggressive self-activity by teachers but also solidarity with other groups of less prestigious workers on campus.

On one occasion, all the campus groups that had organized unions went on strike. The issue for faculty was that the university had reneged on a contract that had been agreed to by its negotiating committee.

Anyone who has experienced such a situation knows how hard it is to rekindle the collective will to take risky action after a dispute has apparently been resolved. At the annual meeting of the Organization of American Historians after Howard's death, one of his colleagues described a meeting of faculty activists the evening they learned of the administration's double-cross. Howard, one of the cochairs of the faculty's strike committee, was not present when the meeting began. The mood was glum. Then Howard appeared, laden with posterboard and markers. A strike went forward. Howard's responsibility, so he says, was "to organize the picket lines at the entrance to every university building, to establish a rotation system among the hundreds of picketers." After nine days of picketing and endless meetings, the university gave in.

Then a second issue presented itself. While teachers were out on strike and walking picket lines, secretaries also struck. For a time "we all walked the picket lines together, a rare event in the academic world." Even after the teachers had signed a contract that banned sympathy strikes, Howard and a few other faculty members urged that teachers refuse to go back to work until the administration agreed to a contract with the secretaries. The teachers as a group could not be persuaded. Howard and four others proceeded to hold their classes outdoors. President Silber threatened them with discharge but, after a storm of protest, backed down.[27]

Howard ended his last class early, then led those in attendance to a picket line in front of the school of nursing.

This deep sense of solidarity with the refusal to quit on the part of struggling families like the one in which he grew up is one reason that persons who knew Howard, either personally or through his books, feel such affection for him. The text that more than any other elicits my own solidarity with and affection for Howard Zinn is the final scene in the first version of his play about Emma Goldman, *Emma*.

Let me paraphrase. A group of aged anarchists have gathered at their favorite Lower East Side café in New York City. Something has stirred the embers. They are actually going to do something: they are going to distribute a leaflet early the next morning.

A man enters the café dressed in a shabby overcoat. Is it possible? Yes! It is Alexander Berkman, released from federal prison after many years of confinement for his attempt to assassinate Henry Clay Frick of U.S. Steel during the Homestead strike.

His comrades crowd around him. Berkman asks: What were you talking about when I came in? They respond: It doesn't matter! This is your first taste of freedom, Sasha! Relax! Be happy!

No, Berkman persists, I want to know. His colleagues answer: Well, if you must know, we are planning a leaflet distribution tomorrow morning. Berkman says: And do you have someone to distribute leaflets at every location where you plan to pass them out? Reluctantly, they admit: For every location except one; we're still looking for someone for Broome Street.

Berkman says: I'll take Broome Street.

And the curtain falls.

Howard Zinn, *presente*.

Part II

Rebuilding the Labor Movement
from Below

Introduction

I have given a good deal of thought to how I could best share my own adventures in doing history from the bottom up.

I began graduate school in 1959. Sit-ins and freedom rides were still in the future; there seemed to be no movement for fundamental social change in the United States. I remember thinking, "What about the period of the American Revolution, when the basic principles of this society were first set forth?" I pursued that question for ten years.

Consensus or Class Conflict?

The big issue among American historians when I was a graduate student was whether the period of the Revolution, and indeed the whole history of the United States, supported the notion that all Americans share the same fundamental values. Those who answered yes were known as "consensus" historians. The older, opposing view, represented by Charles Beard and Carl Becker, was that the Revolution was not only a struggle for home rule but also a contest as to who should rule at home.

I examined farm tenants in Dutchess County, New York (where the town of Poughkeepsie and President Franklin D. Roosevelt's home in Hyde Park are located), and artisans in New York City. What I found was that neither consensus nor class conflict accurately characterized the choices of these economically subordinate groups. Both groups were motivated less by ideology than by economic interest.

Farm tenants wanted to own the farms on which they labored and so supported whichever side in the independence struggle their landlords opposed. Landlords in southern Dutchess County were loyal to the king of England. Their tenants petitioned the New York state legislature to confiscate the estates of these Tories and give or sell the land to the

tenant farmers who worked it. But in northern Dutchess County, where
the largest landlord was a patriot, the tenants rose up in insurrection on
behalf of King George III.

Artisans included well-to-do craftsmen like Paul Revere and less af-
fluent men who fashioned shoes and metal implements, manufactured
sailcloth, drove wagons, and the like. Their position in relation to the
more developed economy of the British Isles was like that of Mexican
corn farmers after NAFTA required Mexico to repeal tariffs on corn
imported from the United States. Before the Revolution, artisans supported whatever might prevent the importation of British manufactured
goods, and after independence they supported a stronger national government with authority to create an effective national tariff. Professor
Robin Einhorn has remarked, "Lynd's arguments about New York tenant
farmers and city artisans became standard in short order."[1]

Arriving in Atlanta to work with Howard Zinn at Spelman College
in the midst of the civil rights insurgency, I tackled the question "Why
didn't the Founding Fathers do more to abolish slavery?"

My most significant effort to answer this question was an article
titled "The Compromise of 1787" that addressed the Northwest Ordinance. It is based on remarks by President James Madison to his secretary Edward Coles that Coles recalled and made public more than forty
years later. Coles implied, and I argued, that the Northwest Ordinance
was not the partial step toward abolition of slavery that is generally supposed. Madison reminded his secretary that many men were members
of both the Constitutional Convention meeting in Philadelphia and the
Continental Congress meeting in New York City, and traveled back and
forth between the two bodies during the summer of 1787, when both
the Ordinance and the Constitution were being drafted. Further, Coles
reported, Madison pointed out that the Constitution and the Northwest
Ordinance contained almost identical language directing that fugitive
slaves be returned to their owners.

Beginning with these initial insights, I discovered that until May
1787, the month that the Constitutional Convention assembled in Philadelphia, the Congress, in drafting statutes for governance of the western
territories of the United States, had assumed that any such statute would
apply to all the western territories, the area roughly delineated by the
Great Lakes on the north, the Mississippi River on the west, and the Gulf
of Mexico on the south. But in May 1787 a plan for that area working its
way through Congress was withdrawn on the brink of passage, and when
an ordinance was next proposed, early in July 1787, it applied only to the
territories north of the Ohio River: the Northwest Territories. What this

meant was that Congress left open the possibility that slavery could expand into the Southwest, that is, into the future states of Alabama, Mississippi, and Louisiana, and beyond them, Arkansas and Texas.

This arrangement had obvious importance for southern plantation owners, who proceeded to create a Cotton Kingdom based on slave labor. It also artificially added, by means of the three-fifths clause in the new constitution, to the projected influence of the South in the House of Representatives and the Electoral College. The case was like that of Conan Doyle's famous story about the racehorse Silver Blaze. What was important was not what the Northwest Ordinance did (prohibit slavery where it didn't make sense economically and wasn't going to happen anyway) but what it did not do (hinder the spread of cotton production by slave labor westward across the South).

Acceptance of my work in the scholarly community has been gratifying.[2] But it does not answer the question that led me to do history to begin with: What help can the past give us in imagining the fundamental change needed by a society that is still racist, still unrepentantly dedicated to capitalism and its global expansion, and still embroiled in seemingly endless warfare?

An Historian "Out of Doors"

At the time of the American Revolution, ordinary persons who could not vote and were not allowed to take part in the indoor work of decision-making bodies were often referred to as the people "out of doors." Roughly in the years 1964–1969 I became a passionate opponent of the Vietnam War and as a result was blacklisted, or, as one might put it, became an historian "out of doors."

I had a last, mountaintop experience in the South as coordinator of Freedom Schools in the 1964 Mississippi Summer Project, then joined Alice and our two children in New Haven, where I was an untenured assistant professor at Yale.

Conflict in Vietnam escalated. I joined Tom Hayden and Herbert Aptheker on a trip to Hanoi in an effort to find some clue that might help in ending that awful war. On my return, the atmosphere at Yale grew decidedly more chilly. The Lynds moved to Chicago. At half a dozen colleges and universities in the Chicago area, the history department offered me a job but the administration vetoed the appointment. I was blacklisted.

In 1973, in my early forties, I started law school. As a lawyer I have encountered industrial workers and high-security prisoners whom I would never have met had I not been pushed out of the Ivy League. And while I did not continue to do research on the period of the American Revolution, I did not stop doing history.

The state of what we called "the Movement" in the late 1960s and early 1970s was precarious. SNCC had collapsed and SDS had splintered. Many courageous young people, having absorbed some version of Marxism, were taking jobs in steel mills and automobile assembly plants. Alice and I encountered a number of persons who had helped workers to organize in the 1930s: three women (the "union maids" of a subsequent documentary movie by that name) and two men who worked for Inland Steel in northern Indiana. Intrigued by their recollections, we decided to collect oral histories from these men and women, and others, who might give some guidance to their younger counterparts who were once again setting out to "colonize" steel mills and automobile plants. My first report on this work, "Guerrilla History in Gary," appeared in *Liberation* magazine in October 1969.

As in my work on Dutchess County and New York City in the era of Revolution, I found that ordinary working people two hundred years later were interested first and foremost in economic survival. However, just as the period of the Revolution also produced a Tom Paine, so in the ranks of the twentieth-century labor movement my wife and I encountered the three women who star in the documentary film *Union Maids* and steelworkers John Sargent, John Barbero, and Ed Mann.

In 1976, Alice and I moved to Niles, Ohio, an industrial suburb of nearby Youngstown. There we lived through tumultuous years in which steel mills were shut down in Youngstown and Pittsburgh and communities struggled to reopen them. Not long out of law school, I served as lead attorney in an effort to open steel facilities that had been shut down. I also sought to be an historian of this effort.[3]

The Lynds retired from Northeast Ohio Legal Services in 1996. Since then, Alice and I have become advocates for the men incarcerated in the new prisons that have been substituted for steel mills in this valley. Five men sentenced to death for their alleged roles in a major Ohio prison uprising have been confined at a nearby "super-maximum security" prison. We have compiled a narrative of that story, too, while also serving as volunteer attorneys for the American Civil Liberties Union of Ohio.[4]

The steel saga represents my longest and deepest immersion in doing history from below. And the steel story is necessarily also a story about the United Steelworkers of America, the AFL-CIO trade union that became the exclusive bargaining representative for workers in basic steel. When Jesse Reese said at a public forum in 1970, "Your dog don't bark no more," he wasn't talking about the company. He was talking about the union. Thus just as my early years in history ended with the question "Why didn't the Founding Fathers do more to end slavery?," so this later inquiry centered on the questions "Why were trade unions in the United States unable to stop corporations from moving manufacturing to other countries, and where does this leave the United States labor movement?"

The following essays span a period between 1969, when Alice and I became acquainted with John Sargent, and 2011, when I took part in a forum at Harvard Law School that looked back on our efforts to prevent the closing of U.S. Steel facilities in Youngstown. I was trying to reach both labor historians and rank-and-file workers; hence, some of the essays have notes and some do not. I have arranged the essays in roughly chronological order in the hope that the interested reader can follow my developing analysis. Whether summarizing the views of contemporary working persons or casting back to forgotten union practice in the 1930s, I was seeking a way out of what Bob Moses of SNCC once described as the "box" in which the institutional labor movement has placed the would-be advocate of fundamental social change.[5]

The Club of Brokenhearted Lovers

For over twenty years there existed in Youngstown an entity that participants called the Workers' Solidarity Club.

The club came about in the following way. Members of a utility workers' local union went on strike and were upset that they received little help from the AFL-CIO Central Labor Union. The local union made its "hall," a room on the ground floor of a two-story building, available for a class that I was asked to teach.

I offered a class common in labor education about how to use the grievance procedure (where a union already existed) or how to file a National Labor Relations Board charge. The following year I was again asked to teach a class, and I decided to dig a little deeper. By this time I had come to know a utility worker named Bob Schindler who was an officer of the local union and who, along with steelworker Ed Mann, provided informal leadership. I asked Bob what the second class should be about. He said, "Whatever you want."

Many of those in the circle of attenders had devoted years of their lives to building local unions and leading direct actions of various kinds. Often they had to face disapproval and discipline from the national unions to which their locals belonged, as well as from the employer. I suggested to the group when we assembled that we should address what

I sensed was a common feeling among us: that something had gone wrong with the mainstream trade union movement. "All of us," I proposed, "are brokenhearted lovers."

At the end of this second series of "classes," the group decided that it did not want to stop meeting, that we should gather once a month as a parallel central labor union. We decided to call ourselves the Workers' Solidarity Club. The felt need was for a place where an individual worker or a group of workers engaged in concerted activity, like a strike, could go for help. We tried to make ourselves available in this way from the early 1980s until Ed Mann's death a decade later, and then, in the form of the editorial board of a newsletter for workers and prisoners, at Bob Schindler's home for another stretch of years until Bob, too, passed on.

The twin sentiments of disillusionment with the mainstream trade union movement and desire for solidarity in resisting profit-maximizing employers thrust themselves on my attention once again as I have been revising this introduction. A group of participants in Occupy Youngstown sat together in the Lynd basement to share our thoughts about how to support the new movement of low-wage workers (see the Afterword at the end of this book). I was astonished at the bitterness with which almost everyone present expressed intense disappointment with a union to which they had either belonged or turned for help.

Then came a long-distance telephone call from a labor organizer whom Alice and I had known for many years, and with whom we had lost touch. He was no longer working for any particular union: he was freelancing for groups that might need his services. He spoke at length and with great emphasis about conclusions to which he had come. National unions, he declared, were useless. They were prepared to give away every hard-earned benefit in the contract as long as they could keep the dues check-off. He felt that workers needed to organize horizontally, place by place, so that when a group of workers went on strike they asked for help from other kinds of workers in the same city, not from some distant national headquarters. He talked about Florida and Wisconsin, truck drivers and teachers. He said that his present perspective was virtually identical with that propounded by the Industrial Workers of the World (IWW) at its founding convention in 1905.

Proposition by proposition, my friend and I had arrived at the same place. The essays that follow tell how I got there.

Guerrilla History in Gary

The history that "has the most influence on . . . the course of events . . . is the history that common men carry around in their heads." Carl Becker wrote this in 1935, repeating his long-standing argument that "everyman [should be] his own historian."

Recently the same idea has appeared in many places. For instance, in his magnificent account of the revolution from below which took place during the Spanish Civil War, Noam Chomsky advises the scholar who wants to tell the truth about that popular movement to talk with the republican exiles still living in southern France.

For labor history the memories which "common men carry around in their heads" are indispensable. They are the primary sources which written records of any kind can only supplement and, when necessary, correct.

The editor of a forthcoming collection of documents on labor history puts it this way:

> American workers have long been invisible men. Long working hours, aborted formal education, fatigue . . . militated against the accumulation of documents so dear to every researcher. The historian of organized labor has the best opportunity to surmount these obstacles, for the existence of a union virtually compels record-keeping. Union files, newspapers, membership records, and minutes provide necessary tangible evidence for a scholar. But reliance upon institutional sources reinforces the tendency to write institutional history. This is precisely why unions have fared so well in the writing of labor history—and why union members are ignored and the overwhelming majority of unorganized workers is barely acknowledged and rarely examined. In fact, if comprehensive efforts are not made now to interview and gather data

from this generation of workers, whether union members or not, future historians will continue to write labor history under the same handicaps that impeded their predecessors.

In view of the current interest in the technique of oral history, it might be thought that the memories of rank-and-file workers were being systematically taped and preserved. Not at all. Oral history, like every other form of American history, proceeds from elitist assumptions. The oral history project at Columbia University had accumulated more than 8,500 hours of taped memories by the end of 1965, but almost entirely from famous individuals. The only significant collection of tapes of the organization of the CIO appears to be 150 interviews with persons who played important roles in the development of the United Automobile Workers, conducted by the Institute of Labor and Industrial Relations at Wayne State University. Ironically, while the incomparable Slave Narrative Collection was being compiled by the Federal Writers' Project, the contemporaneous self-organization of four million industrial workers went unrecorded.

As a result, existing histories of the recent labor movement tend to be both thin and misleading. In an article on "Working-Class Self-Activity," George Rawick comments: "Doubters should listen to the sit-down stories of workers from Flint, Michigan, and compare them to the official UAW history which emphasized the strikes' leadership (none other than the present national officers and executive board of the UAW). Radical scholars should begin to collect materials while there is still time."

Oral history from the bottom up, or as I prefer to call it, "guerrilla history," is of interest to more than radical scholars. Rank-and-file trade unionists want to know the history of the 1930s so that they can respond to the present upsurge of labor militancy armed with an analysis of why the CIO unions so rapidly grew bureaucratic and conservative. (I will present a concrete example of such analysis in a moment.) A second constituency for guerrilla history is the children of working-class families who are going to college so as to avoid going into the mill. Exploration of their own memories and the memories of their parents and their parents' friends can provide, in the words of John McDermott, "the opportunity to discover the reasons for their attitudes on a score of moral and social questions, the reality of their social lives, and the possibility of rebuilding a more humane culture . . . for their own advantage." These young men and women may come to feel, through learning experiences like guerrilla history, that they need not be ashamed of their parents' failure to "make it" out of the factory. Perhaps they will perceive that as teachers or secretaries or health technicians they will still be wage-earn-ers, heirs to a tradition of collective struggle, with roles to play relative to their parents, cousins, brothers, and sisters employed in manual labor.

Finally, there are the radical students and ex-students taking jobs in factories, moving into working-class communities, teaching at junior and community colleges. They need to avoid the missionary attitude so well described by McDermott in his "The Laying On of Culture." For them guerrilla history can be a means of learning at the same time that they teach. As the New Left turns toward labor, guerrilla history can be a valuable tool.

The Wisdom of "Smith" and "Brown"

This summer [1969] I have interviewed perhaps a dozen steelworkers in Gary, East Chicago, and Hammond who helped to organize the first CIO locals in Lake County, Indiana. One man worked on the railroads in Mexico for $22.50 every two weeks before going to work at Inland Steel in 1920. (By the mid-1920s, according to David Brody, more than 10 percent of the steelworkers in the Chicago area were Mexican Amer-icans.) He can remember when steelworkers worked twelve hours a day and a twenty-four hour "double turn" every other Sunday. When he first came to East Chicago he was housed in barracks which had been used by the National Guardsmen who crushed the great steel strike of 1919. The way the CIO purged Communists reminds this old man of the way the Mexican Revolution, after its success, killed Villa and Zapata.

Another man with whom I talked is the son of an activist who was fired after the 1919 strike and was never able to get another job in the mills. My informant's first political act was to join the Gary contingent of the 1931 hunger march. Later he was chairman of the Gary unem-ployed council. He is an apparently inexhaustible source of stories about street-corner meetings broken up by the police and evicted tenants re-stored to their homes by popular action.

With everyone I have raised the question: What happened to the militancy of 1936–1937, when two years of rank-and-file pressure from below finally produced the Steel Workers' Organizing Committee, when half a million workers around the country sat down in their factories, when ten men were shot in the back and killed at the Republic Steel plant near the Indiana-Illinois state line?

The most interesting response thus far has come from two men with a combined experience in their local of more than fifty years. Both be-long to the local's rank-and-file caucus and from time to time have held important offices in the local.

The two men [John Sargent and Jim Balanoff], whom I will call John Smith and Jim Brown, made me aware of the fact that between the failure of the Little Steel strike of 1937 and formal recognition of the United Steelworkers of America in 1942, Little Steel labor bargained with management without written contracts. In the plant employing Smith and Brown, the Steel Workers' Organizing Committee met monthly with the plant superintendent. The workers were represented by grievers in each department, just as they would be after the signing of a contract. (Monthly meetings continued after union recognition until 1950. One of the men to whom I spoke had a complete set of the minutes of these meetings from 1938 to 1950.) But until 1942, as the superintendent himself remarked in the meeting for July 1941, "we have no contract."

Further research revealed that it was just this issue of a written contract which kept labor and Little Steel management apart for these five years. The understanding between U.S. Steel and the Steel Workers' Organizing Committee on March 6, 1937 obligated both sides to meet no later than March 10 to effectuate "a written agreement." According to Tom Girdler, president of Republic Steel and leader of Little Steel management forces, SWOC then demanded that Republic and other Little Steel corporations sign an identical understanding. Republic's refusal to do so initiated the bloody industrial warfare of the following half decade. "The sole remaining issue was that of a signed contract," Girdler states. "The union demanded that we sign the contract and we refused."

Now, what one might term the received version of these events casts SWOC as the unequivocal good guy and Girdler, with his munition stocks and scabs and company police, as indisputably wrong.[1]

Young radical scholars have begun to question this assumption. Mark Naison observes in his study of the Southern Tenant Farmers' Union:

> The CIO built its organizing drive around the recognition of vast industrial unions as the sole bargaining agents of workers in American industries; the great majority of its strikes were fought around the issues of union recognition rather than wages or working conditions. . . . In every instance in which the CIO had extended funds for organization, its goal was to win signed contracts and to institutionalize bargaining on an industry wide level, a basis upon which the CIO could 1) extend its control of wage levels and productive conditions in the American economy and 2) extract a steady income for new organizing.

Not only was the CIO model inappropriate for workers like the Southern tenants who were outside the industrial system and driven by their situation to challenge capitalism politically. In Naison's view, even for industrial workers like those in steel, CIO organizing was a mixed blessing because it sought to assure "a disciplined response by the work force" and "to rationalize a capitalist economy."

My informants Smith and Brown emphatically agree. They go farther. As they see it, the critical difference between the years before 1942 and those that followed was that before signing a contract the workers retained the freedom to strike at any time. In each department, before 1942, the workers had an unwritten understanding with management backed up by the threat of striking. If management was recalcitrant a department would "go down," and in this way, according to John Smith, the 15,000 steelworkers in the plant won things, including wage increases. Both these veteran militants believe that the workers were in a stronger position before a contract was signed. If you must have a contract, adds Smith, it should be as vague as possible and interpreted by the rank and file through their enforcing action.

A Wobbly Perspective

What these men advocate on the basis of their long CIO experience is nothing else than the no-contract position of the IWW. They derive this lesson from the years after the contract was signed as well as from the years before it. Now, says Smith, "you have a pretty good company union." After the signing of a contract the union found itself obligated to police the contract by disciplining members resistant to the pledge "that there shall be no interruptions or impeding of work, work stoppages, slowdowns, strikes, lockouts or other interferences with production and maintenance of the Company's plants during the term thereof." I asked Smith what of the Communist Party's advocacy of a no-strike pledge during World War II. He responded that he was critical of the Communist Party for failing to demand a more democratic structure in the international union, but that, so far as the no-strike pledge was concerned, the fundamental no-strike pledge was that in the contract itself. For instance, in 1948 when Smith was president of the local, members of a department undergoing automation struck to ensure the retention of their jobs at undiminished pay. Over Smith's head the district director of the international union agreed with the company that sixty-five men who had led the wildcat should be fired.

Signing a contract meant not only surrender of the right to strike between negotiations but institutionalization of the dues check-off, which made possible the multiplication of salaried pork-choppers. Before 1942 stewards and grievers were unpaid. They collected dues on the shop floor at the risk of their jobs. Sometimes the local threw up dues picket lines around the mill. Smith and Brown wryly mention a member of "the opposition" in their local who in those days climbed over the fence rather than pay his union dues. Brown himself was fired while dues-collecting, and subsequently blacklisted by four other mills in the area before he got his job back in 1950. Yet he thinks it was better for the local when it had to prove its worth to its members in order to get their dues.

To discover this Wobbly period in the history of one of the more centralized CIO unions, and especially to find that experienced activists look back to that period as the time when they most effectively served their members, seems full of suggestions for organizers seeking to create, or respond to, a new surge of rank-and-file militancy. The Left has not had an effective answer to labor historians who contend that institutional hardening of the arteries is inevitable in any trade union once it begins to demand specific improvements in wages, hours, and working conditions. "Business unionism," it is argued, brings with it a business spirit and a form of organization patterned on the business corporation. For examples of unions which resisted this process we have had to point to unions in marginal sectors of the labor market. Thus one can instance the STFU, which won significant strikes against the cotton growers but, according to its founder H. L. Mitchell, never negotiated with them. But Smith and Brown remember a stretch of about five years when in steel itself a local won concessions from management without surrendering its independence.

Insight spills over into action. Smith and Brown are doubtful whether they can accomplish significant change within the limits set by the structure of the international union and the no-strike clause of the contract. But they are trying, through the rank-and-file caucus. The *Voice of the Rank and File*, the caucus newspaper, proposed the following resolution to a recent convention of the union: "Resolution to Eliminate No-Strike Clause in Contract. The no-strike clause would become inapplicable under the following conditions: (a) If the Company does not abide by the arbitrator's decisions; (b) If the Company delays grievance procedure unduly; (c) If the Company makes arbitrary rules that cause harm to the members." (Clauses b and c would appear to illustrate what Smith means by a "vague" contract!)

In seeking change, Smith and Brown explicitly hark back to the period before the signed contract. Running for chairman of the grievance committee of the local, Smith put out a leaflet which began:

> Used to be a time when if you had a gripe you could get your grievance man, see a foreman and usually get it straightened out. That's out now. The foreman can't settle grievances. The super isn't allowed to settle grievances. Labor Relations (these relations are tougher to get along with than your in-laws) is in the hands of a small group of people who seem to have nothing else to do but figure out ways to skin you out of your rights.

These militants seem to feel a kinship not only with the early days of the CIO but with the IWW. One issue of the *Voice* borrowed language from the Wobblies in urging "that everything possible must be done to settle grievances at the point of production."

"Your Dog Don't Bark No More"

In 1970, the year after I met John Sargent, Charlie McCollester and I organized a forum in three sessions at a community college titled "Labor History from the Viewpoint of the Rank and File."

The speakers at the second session were Jesse Reese and John Sargent. Mr. Reese spoke first, and I have extracted from his remarks only what he said about "your dog," meaning the CIO trade union movement. Then it was Sargent's turn. It was a hot night, and I remember him in the narrow, crowded lecture hall, sweating profusely as he spoke. (He died of a heart attack a few years later.)

In reporting my earlier interview with Mr. Sargent, I referred to "the failure of the Little Steel strike of 1937." At the forum John rejected this characterization, shared not only by trade unionists and labor historians but by labor figures on the Left like Marty Glaberman. According to Sargent, the settlement was "a victory of great proportions." Here he explains why. What workers had won, and made to work for themselves, is what today is called "members only" or "minority" unionism.

Jesse Reese

I want to say, friends, I have to give it to you like it is. The Communists built the union. After we got the union built, something happened to John L. Lewis, and Mr. Philip Murray carried out his aims: he fired every Communist organizer. He made an agreement with the steel trusts, it seems to me, that he would fire the Communists. And that's what happened, and the union's been going back, back, back ever since. It doesn't open its mouth.

55

Today we have in our unions a pet dog—what you might call a pet company dog—led by the caretakers; and the caretakers are the leaders of our union. And our dog is being fed red-baiting and his teeth have been pulled out (that's the no-strike clause) and your dog don't bark no more for you. So the only thing you can get to win now is a cat, and it's got to be a wildcat, organized as a blanket matter. You've got to use blanket cover to keep from being exposed.

Your so-called leaders are the leaders of the industrial pet dog. Your dog don't bark at no misery. Your dog don't bark no more. He can't hear. Makes no difference how many people they kill, your dog don't say nothing. He ain't the dog of 1937, when that dog turned loose nine boys—the Scottsboro Boys—and freed Tom Mooney. Your dog . . . what's the matter with your dog? I couldn't stay in the union, pay dues, and keep quiet. They'd have to do something about things. There's no justice, no justice! And we sit down with a big trade union, with intelligent people (people who are educated, they say), and you don't hear nothing, and you can't say nothing, and you can't see nothing. You can't see those people getting killed. They have declared war on color, and not just on one color, but on all colors from the Kennedys to the Kings to the black ghettos to the Black Panthers to the mine workers. And they're now dancing on the doorsteps of Asia, and your dog don't bark. Because you don't have anything but the pet dog of the steel trusts.

John Sargent

I got in the mills in 1936, and I [was] fortunate to be caught up in a great movement of the people in this country. And that doesn't happen very often in one's lifetime, but it's an experience that I think is important to anyone who has been able to participate in a movement of this kind. It's indeed a very important event in his or her life. Because a movement of the kind that we had in the Steelworkers Union and in the CIO was a movement that moved millions of people, literally, and changed not only the course of the working man in this country but also the nature of the relationship between the working man and the government and between the working man and the boss, for all time in this country. There are some parallels in the movement today, especially among the young people and the black people, that I won't go into. . . .

I was hired at the Inland Steel Company in 1936. And I remember I was hired at 47 cents an hour, which was the going rate, and at a time when there were no such things as vacations, holidays, overtime, insurance, or any of the so-called fringe benefits everybody talks about today.

But the worst thing—the thing that made you most disgusted—was the fact that if you came to work and the boss didn't like the way you looked, you went home; and if he did like the way you looked, you got a promotion. Anything and everything that happened to you was at the whim and the will of the fellow who was your boss and your supervisor. . . . As a matter of fact, in order to get a promotion—and sometimes even in order to work—you had to bring the boss a bottle of whiskey, or you had to mow the boss's lawn, or you had to do something to make you stand out from the other people he saw. This was the type of condition that existed as late as 1936 in the steel mills in this region.

When the CIO came in, the people were ready to accept a change. And because they were ready to accept a change, it was not a difficult task to organize the people in the steel mills. Thousands upon thousands of them, in a spontaneous movement, joined the steelworkers' organization at that time. And they did it because conditions in the mill were terrible, and because they had become disgusted with the political setup in this country and the old tales told by the Republican Party about the free enterprise system in this country in which any man was his own boss, and there was no sense in having an organization, and organizations and unions were anti-American, and so on. All this fell off the backs of the people at that time. They realized that there was going to be a change—both a political and an economic change—in this country, and there was.

John L. Lewis had an agreement with the U.S. Steel Corporation, and they signed a contract. Little Steel—which was Youngstown Sheet and Tube, Republic Steel, Inland Steel, and other independent companies—had no contract with the Steelworkers Union. As a result in 1937 there was a strike called on Little Steel. And one of the things that happened during the strike was the massacre in South Chicago, the Chicago cops beating and shooting the people. The strike was not won. We did not win a contract. Neither Youngstown Sheet and Tube, nor Republic Steel, nor Inland Steel won a contract with the company. What we did get was an agreement through the governor's office that the company would recognize the Steelworkers Union and the company union and any other organization that wanted to represent the people in the steel industry. And we went back to work with this governor's agreement signed by various companies and union representatives in Indiana. At Inland Steel we had a company union; we had our own Steelworkers Union. When we got back to work we had company union representatives and Steelworker Union representatives, and we had no contract with the company. But the enthusiasm of the people who were working in the mills made this settlement of the strike into a victory of great proportions.

Without a contract, without any agreement with the company, without any regulations concerning hours of work, conditions of work, or wages, a tremendous surge took place. We talk of a rank-and-file movement, the beginning of union organization was the best kind of rank-and-file movement you could think of. John L. Lewis sent in a few organizers, but there were no organizers at Inland Steel, and I'm sure there were no organizers at Youngstown Sheet and Tube. The union organizers were essentially workers in the mill who were so disgusted with their conditions and so ready for a change that they took the union into their own hands.

For example, what happened at Inland Steel I believe is perhaps representative of what happened throughout the steel industry. Without a contract we secured for ourselves agreements on working conditions and wages that we do not have today, and that were better by far than what we do have today in the mill. For example as a result of the enthusiasm of the people in the mill you had a series of strikes, wildcats, shutdowns, slowdowns, anything working people could think of to secure for themselves what they decided they had to have. If their wages were low there was no contract to prohibit them from striking, and they struck for better wages. If their conditions were bad, if they didn't like what was going on, if they were being abused, the people in the mills themselves—without a contract or any agreement with the company involved—would shut down a department or even a group of departments to secure for themselves the things they found necessary.

We had an agreement with Inland Steel way back in '38 or '39 that the company would not pay less than any of its competitors throughout the country. We never had it so good, I assure you of that. All you had to do as a union representative was come into the company and say, "Look, we have a group of people working in the pickle line, and at Youngstown, Ohio or Youngstown Sheet and Tube in East Chicago people are getting more money than we're getting for the same job." And if that was a fact, we were given an increase in wages at Inland. In those departments where you had a strong group of union members, where they were most active, we had the highest rates in the country. We were never able to secure conditions of this kind after we secured contracts.

What I'm trying to get at is the spontaneous action of people who are swept up in a movement they know is right and correct and want to do something about. Our union now has a grievance committee of twenty-five people. In those days there were more than twenty assistant grievers and hundreds of stewards. The grievance committee setup could handle the affairs of the people on every shift and every turn with every group. Where you did have contracts with the company (at U.S. Steel, for example) you had a limited grievance procedure. The U.S. Steel plant in Gary, the largest steel plant of the largest company, had a grievance committee of only eleven. Where union officials did not take over the union through a contract with the company (as they did with U.S. Steel), you had a broader, bigger, more effective, and more militant organization that set an example for unions throughout the country. Where the union and the company got together through union contracts (as at U.S. Steel), you had a smaller, more restrictive, less militant union that provided less representation for the people in the mill. U.S. Steel never had a strike (so far as I know) since the union organized, whereas unions like the Inland Steel union had a whole series of strikes in order to protect their conditions and prevent the company from taking over or taking back the things they had earned.

What happens to a union? And what happened to the United Steelworkers of America? What makes me mad, and what makes thousands of other people in the mill mad, is that the companies became smart and understood that in order to accommodate themselves to a labor organization they could not oppose that labor organization. What they had to do was recognize that labor organization. And when they recognized a labor union they had to be sure they recognized the national and international leadership of that labor union and took the affairs of that labor union out of the hands of the ordinary elected officials on a local scale.

Now Little Steel was not smart. Little Steel had people like the president of Republic Steel who said he would go out and pick apples before he would recognize the union. And our own dear Inland Steel Company said they would do nothing, they would rather shut their place down forever than recognize the Steelworkers Union. Now what happened to these companies that did not recognize the union, that forced the union to act against the company, was that the workers developed the most militant and the most inspiring type of rank-and-file organization that you can have. Now when the company realized that this was what was happening, they quickly saw that they had gone off in the wrong direction, and they recognized the leadership of the union.

We used to bargain locally with the Inland Steel Company, and we had our own contract with the company. We let a representative of the international union sit in, but we bargained right in Indiana Harbor and settled our differences right there. But soon Inland began to realize that this was not the way, because they were up against a pretty rough bunch of people who had no ambitions to become political leaders and labor representatives on a national scale. They realized that the best way to handle the situation was to work with the international leadership of this union. And today, the company and the international union get along pretty well.

The union has become a watchdog for the company. The local union has become the police force for the contracts made by the international union. If a local union tries to reject a contract in the Steelworkers Union, the contract is put into effect and the local union acts as the police to see that the men live up to the contract, even if it is rejected by the entire committee [of the local union] which negotiates the contract.

This is, I think, the normal growth which occurs when labor unions and most other organizations become legitimate and old and part of the general situation of the country. At the same time, I think it is important to realize that the growth of the union in this country has changed the bond. We no longer have many of the sweatshops we had in the '20s and early '30s, or the terribly low wages we had before. The union taught the system—taught the industrialists of this country—that it is possible to pay decent wages and provide decent working conditions and still make a fortune. In fact the steel mills make more money now than they ever made before. They do it by paying people a fairly decent wage and by working people not nearly so hard as they were worked in the past. The union has taught the companies how to make money through recognizing the union organization. And the government and the employers have learned how to adopt, co-opt, and engulf the union and make it a part of the establishment. And in making it part of the establishment they took the guts, the militancy, and the fight out of the people who work for a living.

The Possibility of Radicalism in the Early 1930s

The Case of Steel

*John Sargent's interpretation of the degeneration of CIO trade union-
ism turned alternative interpretations upside down. All other analyses,
whether emphasizing Supreme Court decisions, the indirect effects of the
World War II no-strike pledge, or, of course, the Taft-Hartley Act and Mc-
Carthyism, pointed to events that happened after the passage of the Wagner Act and the initial organization of CIO industrial unions.*

*Sargent said, in effect, "No, the problem was the initial pattern of
union recognition and collective bargaining imposed by John L. Lewis on
the incipient CIO." The institutional pattern dictated by Lewis included
the following four elements:*

1. *Exclusive recognition by the employer of a single trade
   union that all persons who survived an initial probationary period and became part of the workforce at a given
   workplace were required to join;*

2. *A clause prohibiting strikes and slowdowns for the duration of the contract;*

3. *A "management prerogatives" clause giving the employer
   sole authority to make major investment decisions, such as*

closing a particular plant;

4. *The dues check-off, whereby the employer deducted union dues from each worker's paycheck and forwarded the money to the union.*

Stunned by John Sargent's insight, I found myself wondering: was there an alternative way to have organized basic industries? The following article reports the initial results of my inquiry.

Recent historians associated with the Left have found industrial union organizing in the 1930s puzzling. We have declined to join in the liberal celebration of its results, pointing to "the partial integration of company and union bureaucracies" in administering CIO contracts (C. Wright Mills)[1] and the CIO's "definition of union organizing that made it impossible . . . to concentrate on political organization that challenged capitalist institutions" (Mark Naison).[2] We have dwelt on happenings which for liberal historians are merely preliminary or transitory, such as the mass strikes in Toledo, Minneapolis, and San Francisco in 1934,[3] the improvisation from below of local industrial unions and rank-and-file action committees,[4] or the many indications of interest in a Labor Party or Farmer-Labor Party.[5]

But this is not enough. In the 1890s, the drive for industrial unionism under Eugene Debs led to a confrontation with a Democratic president, recognition of the need for independent labor politics, and the formation of the Socialist Party. There was a step-by-step transition, first to economic organization on a broader scale, then to political organization, very much in the manner outlined in *The Communist Manifesto*. This did not happen in the 1930s (or at first glance *appears* not to have happened), and we must ask why. I believe there is a connection between the difficulty experienced by New Left historians in answering this question, and the difficulty experienced by New Left working-class organizers. If we had a better idea how radicals should have acted while unions were being organized, we might better understand how they should act today. This essay considers the case of steel.

From 1933 to 1935

When the National Recovery Administration came into existence in June 1933, the feeble AFL union in the steel industry—the Amalgamated Association of Iron, Steel and Tin Workers—reported less than 5,000 workers. By the time of the Amalgamated's annual convention in

1934, its membership had increased to a number variously estimated at 50,000 to 200,000.[6] Harvey O'Connor, then a labor reporter living in Pittsburgh, remembers it this way:

> Along came the New Deal, and then came the NRA, and the effect was electric all up and down those valleys. The mills began reopening somewhat, and the steelworkers read in the newspapers about this NRA Section 7A that guaranteed you the right to organize. All over the steel country union locals sprang up spontaneously. Not by virtue of the Amalgamated Association; they couldn't have cared less. But these locals sprang up at Duquesne, Homestead, and Braddock. You name the mill town and there was a local there, carrying a name like the "Blue Eagle" or the "New Deal" local. These people had never had any experience in unionism. All they knew was that, by golly, the time had come when they could organize and the Government guaranteed them the right to organize.[7]

This remarkable organizing drive was carried out by rank-and-file steelworkers with little help from full-time organizers of the Amalgamated. At the U.S. Steel Edgar Thomson Works in Braddock, for example, an Amalgamated organizer provided membership cards and volunteer organizers from the mill returned in a week with 500 of them signed.[8] Walter Galenson wrongly terms the Amalgamated organizing drive of 1933 "unsuccessful."[9] As a matter of fact, the Amalgamated drive between June 1933 and April 1934 signed up about the same number of steelworkers that the Steel Workers Organizing Committee, using 200 full-time organizers, signed up in a comparable period of time, from June 1936 to March 1937.

The self-organization of the rank and file was at least as effective as the top-down professionalism of the CIO, which had far greater resources at its disposal. Galenson himself quotes Lee Pressman as saying that as of the spring of 1937 SWOC could not have won an NLRB election "on the basis of our own membership or the results of the organizing campaign to date" in either Big or Little Steel.[10] The best testimony to this effect comes from the man who collected SWOC dues, David J. McDonald, later president of the United Steelworkers of America. "Contrary to union propaganda—some of which I helped to write—the steelworkers did not fall all over themselves to sign a pledge card with the SWOC," McDonald states in his autobiography.

What we hoped would be a torrent turned out, instead, to be a trickle. Under our arrangement with the Amalgamated, it would charter a local union as soon as we had enough men signed up in a plant to form the nucleus of an effective organization. Often-times the locals consisted of the half-dozen men daring enough to sign the charter application. When these skeleton requests straggled in, we assigned impressively high lodge numbers in the hope that outsiders would think we had that many locals. Only Murray and I knew how thin the tally was, although Lewis would insist on the truth whenever I visited Washington, then would shake his head in wonderment at the lack of progress.[11]

According to McDonald, SWOC membership was a "shaky 82,000" at the end of 1936, and when U.S. Steel signed a contract in March 1937, SWOC had signed up only 7 percent of its employees.

McDonald offers a hatful of explanations for steelworkers' absence of response to SWOC: a 50-year tradition of nonunionism, the fear of losing jobs, and the fact that some workers "were as apprehensive about dictatorship from an international union as they were of arm-twisting from their employer." Only the last of these makes any sense when one recalls that just three years before the same steelworkers had enthusias-tically organized local unions. The question presents itself: Why did the organizing drive of 1933–1934, strongly supported by the rank and file, fail to achieve the union recognition accomplished by the SWOC drive of 1936–1937 with weaker rank-and-file backing?

The rank and file sought to achieve union recognition through the Amalgamated in 1933, 1934, and 1935. The 1933 effort was the by-prod-uct of a spontaneous strike by coal miners in the "captive mines" of western Pennsylvania owned by the steel companies.[12] These miners joined the United Mine Workers after the passage of the NIRA just as steelworkers were joining the Amalgamated. Late in July, miners at the H.C. Frick mines owned by U.S. Steel struck for recognition of their new UMW locals and the right to elect checkweighmen. UMW president John L. Lewis agreed with President Roosevelt that the men would go back to work and that their grievances would be referred to a special government board. The men refused, their representatives voting 123 to 4 against returning to work for the present. A 44-year-old Irish im-migrant named Martin Ryan emerged as their spokesman. By the end of September 1933, 70,000 miners were on strike.

Then the strike spread to steelworkers. On September 26 miners marched into Clairton, Pennsylvania, where the largest coke plant in the United States made fuel for U.S. Steel mills throughout the Mononga-hela Valley. Hundreds of coal miners and an estimated half of the workforce at Clairton "circled the gates of the Clairton steel and by-products works in endless march, day and night." Meanwhile at Weirton, West Virginia, 50 miles away, 12,000 more steelworkers went out demanding recognition of their new lodges of the Amalgamated. The national president of the Amalgamated, Michael Tighe, declared both the Clairton and the Weirton strike "outlaw."

John L. Lewis and Philip Murray, leaders of the UMW and future leaders of the SWOC and CIO, persisted in attempting to get the miners back to work. O'Connor describes the part played by Murray:

> Vice President Murray of the United Mine Workers summoned the rank-and-file leaders to Pittsburgh. "Today," he warned them, "you are fighting the coal companies; but tonight, if you remain on strike, you will be fighting the Government of the United States. Today you are conducting a strike; tonight you will be conducting a rebellion. Today we may say we are going to defy the greatest friend we've ever had in the history of this nation (President Roosevelt). But I tell you, friends, he can turn against you as strong as he's been for you. He can call out the Army and Navy."

Martin Ryan, leader of the striking miners, answered Murray: "Why do you ask 75,000 men to go back to work instead of telling one man [President Moses of the Frick Company] to sign the contract?" The rank-and-file delegates returned to Fayette County and called 20,000 miners together to consider Murray's back-to-work order. The miners voted to continue their strike until the Frick Company signed a contract.

Finally, on October 30, 1933, Lewis and Murray signed a contract on behalf of Frick's miners with none other than Myron Taylor, the same man who would sign a contract with them in March 1937 concerning steelworkers employed by U.S. Steel. Historians differ as to how much this contract achieved for the miners, but whatever it achieved was thanks to the pressure from below of men who struck without authorization and who refused Lewis and Murray's orders to go back to work. The striking steelworkers achieved nothing. At Weirton, the strikers returned to work with a promise that an election for union representation would be held on December 15. The election turned out to be an election for company-union representatives. In the words of O'Connor: "The grand tactical plan for the united front of steel's mine and mill workers, conceived on the spur of the moment by local rank-and-file leaders in both industries, had been scuttled by a stronger united front, that of Washington, the union leaders, and the steel companies."

The leaders of the Weirton strike, Billy Long and Mel Moore, now joined with other presidents of new Amalgamated lodges to launch a second effort to unionize steel. On March 25, 1934, 257 delegates from 50 of the newly formed lodges met in Pittsburgh to plan strategy for the Amalgamated convention the following month.[13] First among equals was Clarence Irwin, president of the Amalgamated lodge of the Brier Hill works of Youngstown Sheet and Tube, Youngstown, Ohio, and of the Sixth District of the Amalgamated, which included Youngstown, Canton-Massillon-Canfield, and Cleveland.

Irwin is dead now, but Robert R. R. Brooks of Yale University interviewed him in the late 1930s, and further information can be gleaned from a scrapbook in the possession of his wife. Irwin was the antithesis of the demagogue usually placed at the head of crowds by historians. In 1934, at the age of 42, he had worked at steel mills in the Mahoning Valley since 1906, and belonged to the Amalgamated since 1910. He was chairman of the strike committee in his mill during the 1919 steel strike. He was married and had three children. He was a skilled roller and had voted Democratic all his life, except in 1932, when he voted for Norman Thomas.

[In his interview with Brooks] Irwin describes the other rank-and-file leaders as very much like himself:

> Almost all of us were middle-aged family men, well paid, and of Anglo-Saxon origin. Most of us were far better off than the average steelworker and didn't have much to gain from taking part in the movement except a certain amount of personal prestige. Almost all of us could have done better for ourselves if we had stuck with the companies and not bothered about the rest of the men. But for various reasons we didn't.

We were sure, he goes on,

> that the mass of steelworkers wanted industrial unionism, and so did we. But it wasn't clear to us until we set out to get it that we would have to fight not only the companies but our own international officers and even the Government. The process of learning was slow and painful, and a lot of us dropped by the way.[14]

Contrary to John L. Lewis' subsequent allegations, "All these fellows had a union inheritance of one sort or another." Long's father had been a militant in the Amalgamated Association of Iron, Steel, and Tin Workers, and Earl Forbeck's father had been a Knight of Labor.[15] Moreover, the rank-and-file presidents of the new lodges developed the practice of calling together lodge representatives in district conferences. These district meetings had no constitutional standing. They had been used years before for the purpose of informal discussion of common organizational problems, and in the course of time had died out. Now they were revived, at first with the sanction of the national officers, who attended and spoke at many of the conferences. In time more or less permanent officers were chosen for each district.[16]

The March 25 gathering brought together delegates from lodges all over the country. A general strike was in progress in Toledo; the very day the steelworkers met a national strike in auto had been averted; general strikes in Minneapolis and San Francisco were little more than a month in the future. Steelworkers, too, turned to the strike weapon. Delegates decided to take back to their lodges, for proposed presentation to the Amalgamated convention on April 17, the following strategy: All lodges should request recognition from management at the same time; if recognition is denied, a strike date should be set; the Auto Workers, the Mine Workers, and the Railroad Workers should be approached with the idea that these three groups, together with steelworkers, should act together if necessary to gain collective bargaining for any one group. What was envisioned was a national strike, and if need be a national general strike, for union recognition.

The Amalgamated convention adopted this strategy. The convention also adopted resolutions to the effect that the Committee of Ten rank-and-file leaders which had drawn up the strike program should be included in all negotiations arising from it, that no lodge should sign an agreement until all could sign at once, that full-time Amalgamated organizers should be elected rather than appointed, and that the national union should no longer have the power to declare locally initiated strikes unauthorized.[17] The new members of the union appeared to have taken it over from the incumbent leadership.

The rank-and-file leaders understandably found this historic opportunity frightening. "Most of us were capable local or district leaders," Irwin recalls, "but we had very little idea what the national picture was like. . . . We were completely unprepared for a strike. We had no funds, no central leadership, no national organization except the Amalgamated's officers, and they were opposed to strike action." Irwin and his coworkers began to look for help.

They turned first to a group of four intellectuals: Heber Blankenhorn, Harold Ruttenberg, Harvey O'Connor, and Steven Raushenbush. Blankenhorn had edited the Interchurch World Commission report on the 1919 steel strike. He was close to John L. Lewis and Senator Wagner, and later helped to create the LaFollette Civil Liberties Committee. Ruttenberg was a student at the University of Pittsburgh doing research on the steel industry, O'Connor a labor journalist who during this period published *Mellon's Millions*, and Raushenbush an investigator for the Nye Committee.

Appearing at the 1934 Amalgamated convention with a typewriter, Ruttenberg (and O'Connor) assisted the rank-and-file delegates in "putting together the resolutions they wanted the way they wanted them and getting things going."[18] Thereafter they functioned as a behind-the-scenes leadership group cryptically known (because Blankenhorn in particular was concerned lest his association with the rank and file become public) as "The Big Four." "Although they had no money and had to work on the q.t.," remembers Irwin, "[they] gave us something like national leadership. In a way, they were a forerunner of the Steel Workers Organizing Committee."

I believe it is fair to characterize the Big Four (with the partial exception of O'Connor) as Social Democratic intellectuals, in the sense that they had a tendency to rely on publicity and government intervention rather than on the collective power of the workers, and to avoid cooperation with the Communist Party.

But four men with typewriters and connections could not really be the functional equivalent of a SWOC. According to the decisions of the Amalgamated convention, all lodges were to ask for recognition on May 21, and if recognition was refused a strike date was set for the middle of June. On May 7 Irwin wrote to Ruttenberg asking if Ruttenberg could get him the addresses of the men who had led the 1933 strike in the captive mines, and of the leaders of the Steel and Metal Workers Industrial Union (SMWIU).

The SMWIU was one of the dual unions sponsored by the Communist Party during the so-called Third Period of international Communist strategy.[19] It was founded in August 1932 and claimed a membership of 10,000 to 15,000. The SMWIU justly denounced the NRA. It called on working people to rely on their own power rather than on presidential promises, government boards, and so-called labor leaders. By May 1934 it had led local strikes, for instance in Warren, Ohio; East Chicago, Indiana; and Ambridge, Pennsylvania. These had often ended in violent defeat.

After the Warren strike, which led to the discharge of many strikers and the departure from the city of an entire community of Finnish steelworkers, the local Communist Party "was convinced of the impossibility to organize independent labor unions in opposition to the AFL"[20] and sought to persuade William Z. Foster and other national party leaders to abandon dual unionism in steel. The rank-and-file movement in the Amalgamated offered the SMWIU an opportunity to overcome its isolation from the mass of steelworkers. And the SMWIU offered the rank-and-file movement, which had lost its own local strikes at Clairton and Weirton, the national structure and resources so badly needed if a national steel strike were to become a reality.

The difficulty was that in May 1934 the SMWIU had not abandoned the dual unionist line. SMWIU literature urged its members and sympathizers simultaneously "to take the lead in the organization of united committees" to implement the decisions of the convention and to prepare for a strike—and "to build the SMWIU into a powerful organization in their mill."[21] This was a tactic which looked two ways at once. It never will work, and it did not work in the spring of 1934.

Irwin and Ruttenberg arranged a meeting with the SMWIU leadership for May 20. They urged all members of the Committee of Ten and of the Big Four to be there so as "to determine [in Irwin's words] a central plan of attack, set up a central office with a secretary, determine a uniform method of demanding recognition. Find out what help the SMWIU could give us, and discover what the national officers were going to do to bust up our plans." Three days before the meeting, Irwin wrote to Ruttenberg that the only thing which should be sought with the SMWIU was cooperation on the conduct of the strike. That cooperation should be basically through local joint committees which would work in unison even against the orders of the Amalgamated national office, Irwin believed.[22]

Tragically, Irwin was unable to attend the meeting because his wife was seriously ill. He was represented by Ruttenberg, subsequently research director for SWOC, coauthor with Clinton Golden of *The Dynamics of Industrial Democracy*, and steel company executive. Blankenhorn was apparently not at the meeting, but his taped reminiscences make it clear that he was part of the discussion.

> There were telegrams to me, and as a matter of fact I was in Pittsburgh when that meeting was held, and talked with Pat Cush [one of the SMWIU leaders] and the SMWIU boys, and tried to get the brass tacks on it, and in front of them I advised the rank and filers: "If these boys won't walk out of here and keep their mouths shut instead of making public pronouncements, you have no choice but simply to say that they came and saw you but you had nothing to do with them. If they have any paid members to deliver, let them deliver them quietly."

Blankenhorn and Ruttenberg persuaded the rank-and-file leaders not to work with the SMWIU.[23]

Yet responsibility for the failure of the May 20 meeting falls equally on the SMWIU. In contrast to Irwin's proposals for cooperation visible at a local level but behind the scenes nationally, "They [the SMWIU] wanted the rank-and-file group and the SMWIU to issue a joint statement from this meeting, a joint call for a joint convention to focus public attention on the issues, and local organizations to issue joint statements and call joint mass meetings. It was perfectly clear that they wanted to formalize the whole affair, and to be sure that the SMWIU was in the limelight as an organization. As soon as they had withdrawn [from the meeting], the rank-and-file group voted thumbs down on the whole proposition. We'd have been smeared immediately as Communists if we had accepted."

These words from Irwin's interview with Brooks are perhaps more those of Ruttenberg than those of Irwin, who was not at the meeting.[24] But the fact remains that the SMWIU approach counterposed a Left dual union not only to the national structure of the Amalgamated, but also to the local lodges that the steelworkers had built for themselves. Then and later the rank and filers showed themselves quite able to stand up to Red-baiting, and had the SMWIU not placed so much emphasis on its own organization, I believe united action might have been possible. The fact that (to look ahead) the rank-and-file leaders and the former SMWIU leaders easily established a working relationship the following November, after the SMWIU finally abandoned dual unionism, is strong evidence to this effect.

In May and June, after the failure of the May 20 meeting, things went from bad to worse. On May 22 five of the rank-and-file leaders went to the national office of the Amalgamated and demanded $100,000 from the union to help run the strike, the use of the union's printing press, and rooms in the union's building for strike headquarters. They were contemptuously refused. Irwin then proposed to the rest of the Committee of Ten "that we would take over the running of the strike altogether, call upon the lodges for money (my lodge had already put up a hundred dollars), and select a secretary from our group." Only two other members of the Committee supported this leap into the unknown. "I was never so disgusted in my life," Irwin remembers.

At this point the four intellectuals stepped back onto center stage, urging the rank and filers to take their campaign to Washington, where they could attract national press attention and hopefully embarrass the president into intervening on their behalf. Desperate, the rank-and-file leaders agreed. They got the publicity, but killed the possibility of a successful strike. As one of them commented after it was all over, "They spent most of their time in Washington in a futile attempt to 'see Roosevelt.' This running around after Roosevelt created the impression among the steelworkers that a strike was unnecessary, that Roosevelt would step in at the last minute and help them."[25] The precious weeks which might have been used for local strike preparation were squandered, as the national secretary of the SMWIU rightly observed.[26] In the First District of the Amalgamated near Pittsburgh, where more than a thousand steelworkers gathered to support the strike movement on May 27, a meeting a month later, after the strike had collapsed, attracted only 53.[27]

It now appears that in directing the rank-and-file leaders to Washington, Ruttenberg, Blankenhorn, and Raushenbush acted as agents for John L. Lewis. In interviews conducted by the Pennsylvania State Oral History Project in 1968 and 1969, Ruttenberg stated that a steel strike "did not come off because of the intervention of John Lewis and Philip Murray, who counseled against it for fear that an abortive strike would thwart their contemplated plans to move in and really organize the steel industry." The UMW had no contact with rank-and-file steelworkers until spring 1934, Ruttenberg went on.

> At that point they began to exercise influence through myself, and they assigned John Brophy from the UMW to be the liaison man. . . . Blankenhorn was the one who kept telling John Lewis and Philip Murray that they should get control of the rank-and-file committee and use them as a basis for their unionizing work. . . . And so the counsel that I got from Blankenhorn, which I in turn passed on to the steelworkers, was not to strike now because John Lewis was going to come here and have a big organizing campaign that would stand a chance of being successful.

Raushenbush, for his part, "said that we have to show strength among the rank-and-file steelworkers in order to encourage John Lewis to take the risk. . . . And so you had the whole threatened strike and activity to influence John Lewis to come in as well as to influence Congress to pass a National Labor Relations Act."

Through Ruttenberg, Blankenhorn, and Raushenbush, the rank-and-file leaders were brought before Senator Wagner, the sponsor of that act, who "gave them a lecture about not engaging in a premature strike and gave them a lecture that John Lewis was 'going to come in here and do this job right and don't you fellows mess it up.'"[28] Putting this evidence together with Lewis's role during the coal and steel strikes of 1933, the hypothesis suggests itself that if Lewis succeeded in 1937 where the rank and file failed in 1934, it was partly because Lewis did his best to make sure that industrial unionism would come to steel only if he controlled it.

Meantime the steel companies had disdainfully refused to recognize the Amalgamated lodges, and the strike date approached. The companies placed large orders for the purchase of arms and, at least in Gary, arranged to house strike breakers in the mills should a strike occur.[29] As tension mounted the Amalgamated leadership called a special convention in Pittsburgh for mid-June, the time at which, according to the mandate of the convention, a strike date was to be set if recognition had been refused. Reporters, government mediators, delegates, and a confused group of rank-and-file leaders assembled for the convention.

The strategy of the Roosevelt administration, of the Amalgamated leadership, and apparently of Ruttenberg and associates and of John L. Lewis was to have William Green, AFL president, come to the convention and propose yet another government labor board as an alternative to a walkout. Ruttenberg reports on the mood of labor officials and government representatives at the convention: "Social revolution was at hand. Bill Green was their only hope." Clinton Golden was one of three people who met Green at the train and "coached him as to what to say. He said it."[30] The strike was called off. As the news came over the radio in the bars in Braddock, steelworkers tore up their union cards.[31] Ruttenberg also tells us that Irwin got dead drunk and lost the confidence of many delegates, a situation for which Ruttenberg appears to feel he had no responsibility.

There was to be one more effort at unionization by the rank and file, in 1935. During the summer of 1934, Irwin "tried to keep the rank-and-file movement together by supporting the rank-and-file slate of officers that was running in the Amalgamated's fall referendum." In the October 1934 convention of the AFL a resolution was passed urging the AFL executive council to take action in organizing steel. Meanwhile the government board created in June to head off the threatened walkout had done nothing. "Production was picking up," Irwin remembers, "and the steelworkers were stirring again."

More important than any of these events was the fact that—six months too late—the Communist Party abandoned dual unionism. SM-WIU chapters dissolved so that their members could join the Amalgamated. According to Irwin, in November 1934 rank and filers and SMWIU finally got together. Money became available for steelworkers to travel to conferences,[32] and a series of meetings began to heat up the idea of a national strike again. But whereas in the spring of 1934 the Communist Party wanted a steel strike only if the SMWIU could publicly help to lead it, in the spring of 1935 the Communist Party wanted a strike only if expulsion from the Amalgamated could be avoided. Remaining part of the organization they had previously scorned became the primary goal of Party members in steel.

These forces came to a head at a meeting of 400 rank-and-file steelworkers and 100 rank-and-file miners in Pittsburgh February 3, 1935. Our four intellectual friends played their by now familiar role. Ruttenberg wrote to Irwin before the conference warning him of Communist influence, and O'Connor wrote to Irwin after the conference, acting as an intermediary for an unnamed third party in Washington, to urge the rank and file not to act by itself but to consider cooperation with a committee of the AFL executive council to organize steel.[33]

Lewis, too, played a predictable part. Just as Michael Tighe, president of the Amalgamated, threatened to expel from the Amalgamated any steelworkers who attended the February 3 meeting, so Pat Fagan, district director of the UMW, issued similar warnings to dissident miners. After the meeting both men carried out their threats, Fagan stating: "You can't be a member of the UMW and be affiliated with a Red group. That meeting was absolutely Red. Those fellows don't believe in authority or law and order or anything else. They're an asinine crowd of parlor bolshevists!"[34] This is the same Pat Fagan who in April 1936 led a delegation of the Pennsylvania AFL state convention to the national Amalgamated convention nearby and proposed that the Amalgamated accept $500,000 from John L. Lewis and work with him to organize steel.

Ruttenberg, Fagan, and Tighe notwithstanding, the gathering of rank-and-file steelworkers and miners took place as scheduled. It was an extraordinary occasion. Mr. and Mrs. Irwin, Bill Spang, Mel Moore, Roy Hallas, Cecil Allen and Lew Morris represented the rank-and-file leadership in the Amalgamated. Present on behalf of the rank-and-file miners was Martin Ryan, leader of the 1933 strike in the captive mines. The lesson of 1933–1934 had been learned. A resolution was adopted that "the steelworkers know from their own experience that they can secure no help in their struggles from the labor boards or other Federal agencies, but that their only defense . . . is the power of their own organization, exercised by the calling of strikes if and when necessary."[35]

This time, organization was not left to afterthought. A committee was named to open headquarters in Pittsburgh. Local finance committees were to be pressed into service at once. Most remarkable, in view of subsequent history, were speeches by Martin Ryan and (according to the press) numerous other speakers equally denouncing Michael Tighe and John L. Lewis. The one had betrayed the steelworkers and the other

had betrayed the miners, according to the prevailing sentiment at this
meeting. "Lewis and Tighe have crucified you for years," declared Ryan,
"and will continue to do so until you demand and get their resignation
and removal."

Why did these rank-and-file steelworkers and miners fail to press
on toward a national organizing campaign? This time around, the Amalgamated leadership were not going to permit their national convention
to be captured and used to legitimize a rebel movement. Within days
of the February 3 meeting Tighe expelled the lodges represented there.
What was critical was the rank and file's response to the expulsions.
Here the Communist Party, with its newfound concern for labor unity,
and John L. Lewis, jockeying in Washington for passage of the Wagner
Act and Guffey Act, again had determining influence.

The expelled lodges represented the overwhelming majority of the
Amalgamated membership.[36] They might simply have declared that they
were the Amalgamated, or reorganized as federal unions directly affiliated with the AFL, and in either case proceeded to organize steel. It
appears that many members of the rank and file movement—the rank
and file of the rank and file, so to speak—wanted to do this. O'Connor
reports that at the February 3 meeting "some difficulty was experienced
in stemming the apparently powerful sentiment of many delegates . . .
that an independent union should be started now."[37]

An independent union was exactly what the Communist Party had
been trying to build the year before but now no longer desired. The resources which might have financed an organizing drive were used instead to campaign for reinstatement in the Amalgamated. The National
Organizing Committee set up by the February 3 meeting distributed
50,000 leaflets in April calling for "Unity For All Steel Workers." "Our
program," the leaflet stated, "is the restoration of unity in the union and
the organization of the unorganized steel workers."[38] Lawsuits followed
to compel Tighe to reinstate the expelled lodges. These were successful and on August 1, 1935, it was announced that unity had been re-
stored. In the meantime, however, another strike threat had swelled up
and been dissipated, with the result that the Amalgamated, to which
the expellees won reinstatement in midsummer 1935, had by then been
reduced to the empty shell it was two years before.

In dissipating the strike threat of 1935, Lewis's misleadership sup-
plemented the misleadership of the Communist Party. Early in March
a meeting to implement the February 3 decisions was held in Weirton,
attended by steelworkers from Illinois, Indiana, Ohio, Pennsylvania,
and West Virginia. Conference speeches, the Federated Press reported,

showed great sentiment for a strike in steel. Clarence Irwin reported that "the kind of union we are going to have will not depend on courts, but on organization and the picket line."

Later that month, William Spang, president of District 1 of the Amalgamated, tied a steel strike to a strike of 400,000 soft coal miners threatened for April 1. "Rank-and-file committees of steel workers and coal miners have been meeting to set up plans to strike April 1. If the United Mine Workers of America does not get a new contract, both unions will join in united strike action," Spang said. He added: "We have decided to disregard all arbitration boards. . . . There is only one way we can win our demands—by an industry-wide strike. That's just what we're building up for now."[39]

But there was no coal strike April 1. On the eve of the miners' walkout, John L. Lewis postponed action till June 16 "out of consideration of the President of the United States and the National Industrial Recovery Board."[40] On Memorial Day 1935, just two years before the Memorial Day strike sacred in CIO annals, the steel strike almost happened from below.

What at first seemed to the Federated Press "the long-expected clash in the steel industry" began in Canton, Ohio. "Rank-and-file leaders led it; not one union-paid official had a directing hand in it," Ruttenberg wrote. The strike began at the Berger Manufacturing Company, a wholly-owned subsidiary of Republic Steel employing 450 persons. An AFL federal union at the plant struck to enforce a government finding that the company was refusing to bargain collectively. Two hundred fifty thugs attacked the strikers with teargas and lead pipes. One striker, Charles Minor, had the side of his face torn off, and in all 14 persons were hospitalized. As so often in those years, this picket-line brutality triggered a general strike. Within 24 hours 4,000 Republic Steel employees in the Canton area had walked out in protest, led by Lewis Morris, one of the Committee of Ten of 1934.

Two other members of the Committee from nearby communities, Mel Moore from Clairton and Clarence Irwin from Youngstown, apparently tried to call a national strike. On May 29 they asked "all Republic mills to send delegates to Canton to formulate plans for spreading the strike nationally." On May 31 "The Central Strike Committee (in Canton) issued a call for support from all lodges of the Amalgamated." The only response, or parallel action, that has come to light was by Bill Spang's Fort Dukane Lodge in Duquesne, Pennsylvania. There a strike at the U.S. Steel mill was called for 3 p.m. May 31, but short-circuited when Spang and other officers of the lodge were arrested for parading without a permit. Meanwhile in Canton an attempt to spread the strike to neighboring Massillon collapsed when nonunion employees flooded the Amalgamated lodge meeting and voted not to go out. County and city police broke up the Canton picket lines, and the men started back to the mills.[41]

Once more the rank and file looked to the UMW. "Following Spang's release, the Fort Dukane lodge decided at a mass meeting to issue a call to other lodges to 'strike all Carnegie Steel Company [U.S. Steel] mills June 16,' the date set by the United Mine Workers of America for its strike in the bituminous fields." But Lewis postponed this strike too. On June 14 he promised President Roosevelt not to strike until June 30 so that Congress could act on the Guffey bill. On July 1 the coal strike was postponed for a third time, and on July 29 for a fourth. Meanwhile on July 5 the Wagner Act became law, and late in August the Guffey Act, setting up NRA-like machinery for the coal industry, finally made it through both houses of Congress.[42]

Conclusion

Two philosophies of industrial union organization expressed themselves in these events. Lewis's approach stressed governmental intervention so as to make a "responsible" unionism which would avoid strikes. As Len DeCaux summarized it at the time, Lewis and a number of other union officials told the Senate Education and Labor Committee considering the Wagner Act: "Allow the workers to organize, establish strong governmental machinery for dealing with labor questions, and industrial peace will result." DeCaux noted that some employers favored this approach, and that the expectation in Washington of international war made its adoption more likely.[43]

The second approach relied on strike action, and insisted on writing the right to strike into any labor-management contract which resulted. No one can prove that a national steel strike in 1933 or 1934 would have been any more successful than the defeated national steel strike of 1919. Yet it was Blankenhorn's retrospective judgment that "without even the pretense of Amalgamated leadership" the rank-and-file movement would have involved 75,000 to 150,000 steelworkers in a national strike; and O'Connor argued at the time that any strike in steel was likely to reach a climax within a few weeks, because the Government could not allow it to continue "in view of the restiveness of workers in the auto industry and other industries."[44]

Seeking proof in the experience of SWOC, one can argue that the Little Steel Strike of 1937 shows what would have happened had steelworkers struck in 1934 or 1935. But one can also argue that SWOC would never have gotten its contract with U.S. Steel in March 1937 had auto workers for General Motors not been willing to strike and occupy their plants just previously.

The trade-union line of the Communist Party after mid-1934 dove-tailed neatly with the approach of John L. Lewis. The Party maneuvered brilliantly within the skeleton Amalgamated to have Lewis offer $500,000 to the Amalgamated for a steel drive, with the understanding that the money would be administered by Lewis, and to have the Amalgamated accept that offer.[45] When SWOC was formed, the Party made available 60 organizers.[46] The rank-and-file dream passed into the hands of Lewis in the bastardized form of an organizing committee none of whose national or regional officers were steelworkers, an organizing committee so central-ized that it paid even local phone bills from a national office, an organizing committee, in DeCaux's words, "as totalitarian as any big business."[47]

It could have been otherwise. The critical weakness of the rank and file was its inability to organize on a national scale. Had the Commu-nist Party thrown its organizers, its connections, and its access to me-dia, lawyers, and money in a different direction, there might have come about an industrial unionism not only more militant and more internal-ly democratic, but also more independent politically.

Coming about as it did, industrial unionism in steel lacked any thrust toward independent political action. By 1935 the rank-and-file leaders had lost confidence in the "National Run Around" and, to a con-siderable degree, in President Roosevelt. Experience daily brought more and more workers to the position that "we are through forever with Washington" (Mel Moore), "we're through with weak-kneed appeals to government boards" (Clarence Irwin).[48] They were prepared to defy the national government through strike action and to seek parallel strike ac-tion from workers in other industries. In effect they wanted to duplicate Minneapolis, Toledo, and San Francisco on a national scale. And despite Roosevelt's genius in letting local Democrats take the onus of state ac-tion against striking workers, a national steel strike might have brought steelworkers into collision with Roosevelt just as a national rail strike had brought Debs into collision with Cleveland in 1894.

Even as it was, there were indications of support among steelwork-ers for independent political action. In 1935, along with many other unions in that extraordinary year, the Fort Dukane and South Chicago lodges of the Amalgamated passed resolutions for (in the South Chicago wording) an "anti-capitalist labor party."[49] In 1936, Clarence Irwin stated that "I am in favor of a real Labor Party with no connection with any of the existing parties." The last clipping in his scrapbook describes a 1939 regional SWOC meeting which passed a motion stating: "Whereas labor's experience in the political field has been anything but satisfactory, therefore be it resolved that our ultimate goal be the fostering of a third party called the Labor Party."[50] Given the existence of this sentiment, at the very least it should have been possible to organize local labor parties which, after the death of Roosevelt in 1945, could have joined to form a deeply rooted national third party.

But industrial unionism came to steel and to the CIO generally under the auspices of a longtime Republican who at no time favored a national third party, and of a national radical party which, by mid-1936, was uncritically supporting the incumbent Democratic President. The new industrial unions lost little time espousing the political company unionism of the two-party system.

Local 1330 v. U.S. Steel
(1977–1980)

As of the time the Lynds moved to Youngstown in 1976, analysis from below had suggested that the CIO pattern of collective bargaining gave management the authority to make unilateral production decisions, including the decision to shut down an entire plant, while at the same time taking away from labor, by means of the no-strike clause, the opportunity to respond by direct action. A second tentative conclusion, based on efforts to organize the steel industry in 1933–1935, was that a more democratic, horizontal style of organizing had been possible but failed to materialize because of the difficulty of coordinating local initiatives nationally.

Reality soon reinforced these hypotheses. The first of three major steel complexes in Youngstown closed abruptly in September 1977. Efforts to do something about it through the grievance process or by filing a National Labor Relations Board charge were frustrated by the management prerogatives clause in the Basic Steel Contract.

Steelworkers (not lawyers) suggested a way around the management prerogatives clause. They pointed out that U.S. Steel spokespersons in Youngstown had repeatedly promised that their facilities would stay open as long as they made a profit. Lawyers at the local Legal Services office believed it might be possible to argue that the company had made a second contract with its Youngstown workers, separate from the Basic Steel Contract and enforceable in court. A lawsuit was filed.

As lead lawyer in the litigation, I found myself turning to oral history to establish the facts necessary to support our legal theory. Here is the story as I told it at Harvard Law School thirty years later.

Background

Youngstown, Ohio, had the unusual experience that in each of three successive years—1977, 1978, and 1979—the closing of a major steelmaking complex was announced. By the summer of 1980 steel was no longer being made at what had been, at one time, the second or third largest steelmaking community in the United States.

With each shutdown announcement the community's understanding deepened. When the closing of the Campbell Works was announced in September 1977, popular sentiment blamed the federal government for imposing unreasonable environmental standards and for letting foreign steel into the country. Announcement in 1978 that Brier Hill would be shut down caused local public opinion to target the Lykes Steamship Company, a corporate conglomerate that had acquired Youngstown Sheet & Tube and, so it was said, used the steel company as a "cash cow" for additional acquisitions. The final closings, announced by U.S. Steel in November 1979, resulted in dramatic direct action and in litigation in which I served as lead counsel.

In law school I had been fascinated by the concept of "promissory estoppel." The idea was that if A made a promise to B, and B, with A's knowledge, acted in reliance on that promise to his detriment, this course of conduct gives rise to an enforceable legal contract.

I was accordingly delighted when, after U.S. Steel announced the closing of all its Youngstown-area facilities, my Legal Services colleague Jim Callen remarked: "The newspaper say the workers believe they had been promised the mill would stay open. Isn't that promissory estoppel?"

Tape recorder in hand, I set off to interview steelworkers up and down the Mahoning Valley to find out exactly what they had been promised, and whether U.S. Steel had broken that promise when it closed the mills.

Had U.S. Steel made a promise? David Roderick, chairman of the board of the corporation, had stated on local television in June 1979, less than six months before the company announced the shutdown, "We have no plans for shutting down . . . Youngstown." More specifically, Youngstown area superintendent William Kirwan had promised members of the local unions that so long as the Youngstown facilities made a profit they would not be closed. On the eve of trial I was able to take a deposition from Superintendent Kirwan. He confirmed that he had offered that assurance on the mill "hotline."

Next, had the workers relied on that promise to their detriment? Frank Georges, a 37-year-old machinist at U.S. Steel's Ohio Works, told me that after hearing Mr. Roderick and Mr. Kirwan he and his wife had decided to buy a larger house so as to be able to invite his wife's parents, who were ill, to live with them. Mr. Georges had spent most of November 27 at a local bank completing the "closing" on the new home. As he drove home from the bank Mr. Georges was obliged to stop at a railroad crossing. He turned on the car radio and heard that the mill was to be closed.

At his deposition Mr. Kirwan also shared with us a glossy brochure he had prepared for his corporate superiors outlining plans to make the Youngstown mills more profitable. The existing situation was that in its Ohio Works, across the Mahoning River from downtown Youngstown, U.S. Steel made molten steel in open hearth furnaces. The hot metal was then put in railroad cars and transported seven miles upstream to the company's McDonald Mills where it was reheated and rolled into finished coils. Superintendent Kirwan's idea was to build electric furnaces next to the finishing mills. Besides making it possible to produce the steel more efficiently, this strategy would eliminate the costly transportation and reheating of the semifinished steel. The brochure had a red light and a green light on its outside cover. The idea, so said the brochure, was to press the green light on the electric furnaces at the same time that the company pushed the red button on the open hearths, continuing production and filling orders "without missing a beat."

Newly armed with this exciting information, we proceeded to trial. The plaintiffs were six local unions, several dozen individual steelworkers, an organization called the TriState Conference on the Impact of Steel, and the incumbent Republican Congressman. In addition to the main claim of promissory estoppel, the suit alleged a community property right had been infringed—a kind of public easement to prevent the wasting of property—and an antitrust claim over the refusal of U.S. Steel to sell the plant to the workers.

Trial was held in the old courthouse near the river in early March. Every day at lunchtime, lawyers for workers and the supportive crowd of those in attendance would meet in a church across the street. We made plans to ring the church bells of Youngstown if we won.

We lost. I stayed up all night before final argument working on my remarks. As I presented them the next morning there was a hush in the courtroom, and when I returned to the table around which sat the presidents of the plaintiff local unions, I could feel their support. Even the judge, as we met on the way to the men's room during a bathroom break, said to me: "Great closing, Staughton." Then, after lunch, he read a long typewritten opinion that had to have been written the night before.

An appeal followed. The opinion of the federal appeals court began with the words, "This appeal represents a cry for help from steelworkers and townspeople in the City of Youngstown who are distressed by the prospective impact on their lives and their city of the closing of two large steel mills . . ." The Court went on to quote from appellants' amended complaint the many representations by U.S. Steel to the workforce at its Youngstown mills that the facilities would remain open so long as they were "profitable." There followed an arcane discussion of the meaning of the word "profit" in which the Court followed the definition offered by U.S. Steel executives at trial rather than that which Mr. Kirwan, the corporation's highest-ranking officer in the Youngstown area, had communicated to the local unions and their members. A community property claim was also found wanting on the ground that only a legislature, not the courts, could formulate public policy "on the great issues involved in plant closings and removals." Finally the appeals court, acting out of "perhaps an excess of caution," remanded the antitrust claim to the District Court, where it, too, died.

Analysis

There is a tendency to look back on events like the Local 1330 law suit as beads on a long string of labor struggles, some of them won, most of them lost, all of them inspiring.

Let me suggest a different conceptual framework. I believe that the shutdown of steelmaking in Youngtown and then in Pittsburgh illustrates the catastrophic failure of the CIO model of trade unionism. It is a failure comparable to the collapse of European Social Democracy in August 1914 when labor parties in nation after nation voted to support taxes for the war efforts of their various governments.

From the 1970s onward, industrial trade unions in the United States with hundreds of thousands of members have stood by helplessly as corporations shut down manufacturing and moved their operations to other countries. This is not the typical recession followed by the return of manufacturing to previous levels. Corporations are hiring again, but overseas. Thus more than half the 15,000 workers that Caterpillar, Inc. hired in 2010 were hired outside the United States. Corporations are expanding markets, but in other countries. Thus in 2010 General Motors sold 2.2 million vehicles in the United States but 2.4 million vehicles in China. And the percentage of American workers in trade unions declined to 11.9 percent in 2010, "the lowest rate in more than 70 years."

We in the law tend to think of any defeat as a failure to pursue the appropriate legal theory. However, we had good legal theories in Youngstown and Pittsburgh. In Youngstown we pursued a contract theory, promissory estoppel, articulated in the Restatement of Contracts 2nd section 90. In Pittsburgh close to a dozen municipalities in the Monongahela Valley, including the City of Pittsburgh, created a new regional entity similar to the Tennessee Valley Authority and sought to acquire, reopen, and operate shutdown steel mills by using the power of eminent domain.

We failed, not because our legal theories or our lawyering were inadequate, but for several more fundamental reasons.

First, the United Steelworkers of America sabotaged our efforts. The USWA was suspicious of any initiative that it did not control. In Youngstown, the so-called international union left the battle to its local unions, disavowed the idea of worker-community ownership, and failed even to file a requested amicus brief when we appealed to the Sixth Circuit Court of Appeals. In Pittsburgh, the international relied on feasibility assessments by the Wall Street firm Lazard Freres and failed to inform embattled rank and filers until long after it had ceased to believe in and support their cause.

Second, without the support of the Steelworkers, we failed to obtain from the federal government an indispensable component of any legal strategy for reopening facilities as capital-intensive as steel mills, namely, money. A Democratic Party administration abandoned Youngstown. At the time it would have cost perhaps twenty million dollars to acquire any of the closed facilities in the Mahoning Valley. But every ton of steel in Youngstown was made in antiquated open hearth furnaces. It would have made no sense to reopen any of the area's steel mills without the capacity to rebuild the "hot end," that is, to install Basic Oxygen or electric furnaces in place of open hearths, and substitute continuous casters for blooming mills to semifinish the steel. In any of the three mills that shut down in Youngstown between 1977 and 1980 necessary new investment would have cost at least two hundred million dollars. But the Carter Administration had set aside loan guarantees to assist steelmakers amounting to only one hundred million dollars for the entire country. As John Barbero observed in the documentary film *Shout Youngstown*, decisionmakers in government and private industry were not interested in worker-community steel operations in what they considered their private preserve.

In Pittsburgh, the struggle unfolded during the first years of the Reagan Administration. The exercise of eminent domain has two prerequisites. The first is a public purpose. The second is cash in the amount of fair market value. Where were the TriState Conference on the Impact of Steel or the newly minted Steel Valley Authority to find that kind of money in the early 1980s?

Finally, the union reform movement, even had it been more successful, would not have prevented this Rust Belt catastrophe. That movement had focused on the internal government of unions; hence, between 1970 and 2000 the campaign of Arnold Miller and Miners for Democracy in the United Mine Workers, of Ed Sadlowski in the United Steelworkers of America, of Ron Carey and Teamsters for a Democratic Union in the International Brotherhood of Teamsters.

None of these reformers said anything about two features of the standard CIO collective bargaining agreement that made our task in Youngstown and Pittsburgh almost impossible.

The first such feature is the management prerogatives clause. One day during the summer of 1980 I stopped by the Local 1330 union hall. This was the meeting place from which Ed Mann had led a mass meeting of outraged steelworkers "down that hill" to occupy the U.S. Steel administration building. Six months later, defeat was visibly evident. The now empty building with its big glass windows had become a natural target for neighborhood kids, and several windows and the glass front door had been smashed.

Bob Vasquez, president of Local 1330, was alone in the building, sorting papers. He looked up as I came in and said, "I understand that you're a historian." Then he gave me several typewritten drafts of the first collective bargaining agreement between the Steel Workers Organizing Committee and U.S. Steel.

One clause was the same in all these drafts, and remains virtually unchanged today, seventy-five years later. It read:

> The management of the works and the direction of the working forces, including the right to hire, suspend or discharge for proper cause, or transfer, and the right to relieve employees from duty because of lack of work or other legitimate reasons, is vested exclusively in the Corporation.

Having thus given management a free hand to make unilateral investment decisions, including the right to close a facility "because of lack of work or other legitimate reasons," the new CIO unions also took away from their members the ability to do anything about such decisions by direct action. A second feature of the standard CIO collective bargaining agreement, for example in the contracts with General Motors and U.S. Steel in early 1937, was the clause prohibiting strikes and slowdowns for the duration of the contract.

The no-strike clause violated the explicit legislative intent of the Wagner Act, expressed in Section 13 of the statute. The principal draftsperson of the National Labor Relations Act, Leon Keyserling, was asked by an interviewer years later whether "there was some special reason for putting that residual guarantee of the right to strike in the Act." Keyserling responded:

> There was a definite reason. First, because Wagner was always strong for the right to strike on the ground that without the right to strike, which was labor's ultimate weapon, they really had no other weapon. That guarantee was a part of his thinking. [And it] was particularly necessary because a lot of people made the argument that because the government was giving labor the right to bargain collectively, that was a substitute for the right to strike.

Keyserling added: "We didn't want to interfere in any way with that basic weapon. We never interfered with the right of the employer to close his plant."

Keyserling's apprehension proved altogether correct. Proceeding on the fiction that rank-and-file members had somehow voluntarily surrendered or "waived" their statutory right to strike during the duration of a collective bargaining agreement, unions, the NLRB, the courts, and professors of labor law have acquiesced in this dramatic departure from legislative intent.

So what is to be done? Let me suggest a radical tactic and a radical strategy.

A Radical Tactic

The radical tactic is an extension of management's duty to bargain embodied in Section 8(a)(5) of the Act to encompass what have been called "members-only" or "minority" unions, that is, any group of workers numerically fewer than half the potential voters in an appropriate bargaining unit. Professor Charles Morris, in his book *The Blue Eagle at Work*, demonstrates that this was the original conception of union recognition in the 1930s and recommends a duty to bargain with members-only unions as a way to reclaim meaningful democratic rights in the American workplace.

An important ambiguity remains, however. Existing unions have at all times, in Professor Morris' words, "looked upon these membership-based agreements as merely a temporary means" to the end of exclusive representation, "useful stepping-stones on the path to majority membership and mature collective bargaining."

This was spectacularly true of the CIO's Founding Father, John L.

Lewis. Lewis, while apparently endorsing a members-only approach as a preliminary objective in newly organized workplaces like the Denver tramway system or the nation's steel mills, fought it bitterly within his own union, the United Mine Workers. Indeed Lewis' hostility toward members-only unionism for coal miners was the reason the American Civil Liberties Union opposed the Act.

Cletus Daniel tells the story in his book *The ACLU and the Wagner Act*. The ACLU's misgivings sprang from deep involvement in a bitter jurisdictional dispute between two rival unions in the bituminous coal fields of southern Illinois. In late 1932, dissident local unions had bolted District 12 of the UMW to form the Progressive Miners of America. When the National Industrial Recovery Act (NIRA) was enacted in June 1933, [Roger] Baldwin feared

> that Lewis would succeed in having included in the bituminous coal code labor provisions giving the UMW exclusive bargaining rights, employer checkoff of union dues, and a closed shop. Baldwin was convinced that such a development would surely threaten the destruction of the Progressive Miners and thereby, deny the right of thousands of miners in Illinois to be represented by a union of their own choosing.

One concludes that members-only unionism as a stepping stone to exclusive representation would be unlikely to usher in the new day imagined by Professor Morris. But what about members-only unionism as a permanent arrangement, that is, a situation as in Europe where different unions exist in the same workplace?

I recently experienced a moment of enlightenment in this regard. The very first labor activist with whom I did oral history was John Sargent, three-time president of the local union at Inland Steel in East Chicago, Indiana. Labor historians generally describe the Little Steel Strike of 1937 as a defeat in contrast to the agreement with U.S. Steel earlier that same year. John Sargent, however, called the end of the Little Steel Strike "a victory of great proportions" as a result of which "we secured for ourselves . . . working conditions and wages . . . that were better by far than what we have today." How could this be? What in the world was John talking about?

John Sargent was describing members-only or minority unionism that, in his experience, was more effective than the exclusive representation that superseded it during World War II. . . . Nick Migas, grievance committeeman in the critical open hearth, recalled an incident when the company refused to settle a grievance for the charging car operators. "So that night it started to slow down, and by the next morning there were two furnaces where they had to shut the heat off. They settled the grievance in a hurry. Nobody told anybody to strike. There was just that close relationship, working with the people, where they knew what was necessary."

So what would a workplace be like if members-only unionism became a permanent way of life? It would be interesting to find out. Rank-and-file workers would presumably retain the right to protest an unjust discharge or a shutdown decision when, where, and how they thought best. There would be no deduction of dues from a worker's paycheck unless authorized by that member, and so, as Morris writes, the union's accountability to voluntary members would be governed by ordinary principles of agency. Finally, that which outside the workplace is viewed as a prerequisite to democracy, an opposition party or parties, would be available if desired.

But this radical tactic remains a tactic. Like other radical tactics such as working to rule or occupation of the plant, except in an unusually favorable context and after life-and-death struggle it would not have prevented U.S. Steel from shutting down its Youngstown mills at will. We need a strategy.

A Radical Strategy

This is where Pittsburgh, not Youngstown, and Local 1397, not Local 1330, came forward as pioneers and showed the way. The Pittsburgh movement in the first half of the 1980s fought tooth and nail for worker-community ownership, just as Youngstown had. But Pittsburgh pursued a strategy based on eminent domain. I want to stress two things about that strategy.

First, we didn't say: "We are socialists who believe in public ownership, and therefore, U.S. Steel, get out of the way." Instead we said: "If U.S. Steel won't make steel here in [whatever community it was], we will." And: "If [facility X] cannot return a rate of profit acceptable to U.S. Steel shareholders, we'll run the plant as long as we can cover our expenses."

And second, it is pure fiction to suggest that American workers threatened with the alternative of a plant shutdown would reject such an approach. Frank O'Brien was president of the local union at the big Jones & Laughlin steel mill on the north side of the Monongahela River. He also served in the Pennsylvania legislature, where he saw the way employers used the eminent domain power. Let me close with these words of Frank's:

When you work in a mill, and you see all these guys with the know-how, all together right there, then you see that you have the ability to operate the mill no matter what top management does.

The company says, "Hey, it's not profitable for us any more to produce steel here." But we still need jobs. Companies like J&L are making money. They are moving because they don't make *enough* money to suit them. They've let their plants run down like an old automobile: you run it into the ground, and then you take the license plate off and walk away from it.

So we should think about forming an Industrial Development Authority and running the mills ourselves. . . .

The companies have used [eminent domain] . . . for their own purposes. In the 1950s J&L used to evict people from their homes in Scotch Bottom in Hazelwood. They said they needed the land to expand, but when they had evicted the people and gotten the land they didn't expand. They just let the land sit there and stored raw materials on it.

So I'm thinking the law can be used in reverse.

I think back to the time when the Port Authority was born. Pittsburgh Railways was the big operator transporting people in the City of Pittsburgh. They ran into a financial bind. So the Port Authority was formed, taking in all the bus companies in Allegheny County as well. It bought up the railway and the bus companies because people still had to be transported.

Recently they decided to close down the J&L hot strip mill. A thousand people lost their jobs.

A couple of Sundays later the Mayor was out to our father-and-son communion breakfast at St. Stephens in Hazelwood. He made a little speech and then he opened it up for questions.

So I got up. I said the Mayor had better start worrying now about the U.S. Steel mills.

He said, "Well, what would you do?" I told him, "You, and the County Commissioners, sit down and form an authority, like the Port Authority. We can run the mills ourselves."

"We Are All We've Got"

Building a Retiree Movement in Youngstown, Ohio

Introduction

On July 17, 1986, LTV Steel Company, the second-largest producer of steel in the United States, declared bankruptcy and immediately cut off health and life insurance benefits for approximately forty-eight thousand retirees. Within days, retirees of steel mills in and around Youngstown, Ohio, formed an organization called Solidarity USA to fight for promised pension and medical benefits.

LTV's decision to stop paying medical insurance claims when it filed for protection under Chapter 11 of the Bankruptcy Code had catastrophic results. Retiree Roy St. Clair came home from the hospital on July 17. He spent a day frantically seeking alternative medical insurance. When he experienced a recurrence of his heart symptoms, he did not seek hospitalization because he did not know how he could pay the bill. He died a few hours later.

Delores Hrycyk, a lector in her Catholic church and wife of a retiree with thirty-six years at Republic Steel, telephoned radio talk shows and called a rally in downtown Youngstown for Saturday, July 26. A thousand people attended.

Several days later, hundreds of Youngstown-area retirees, under Hrycyk's leadership, met in a Youngstown suburb to form an organization. The suggestion was made from the floor that the group resembled Polish Solidarity. That's right, Hrycyk responded. Thinking out loud, she added, "Let's call it Solidarity USA."

The Attorneys' Story

Our office was overwhelmed with clients coming in and phoning. One woman told us she had enough heart medicine for fifteen days, and when that ran out she could not afford to buy more.

We are not bankruptcy lawyers. We could not get the help we needed from people who were bankruptcy lawyers. Many of the questions having to do with medical and life insurance were outside their experience. Our questions were not ones where there was already black-letter or established law.

Alice asked a bankruptcy lawyer whether a hospital bill incurred after the bankruptcy by a person who retired before the bankruptcy was a postpetition or a prepetition debt. The obligation to pay arose prepetition, but there was no way to know prepetition whether or when the hospitalization would occur or what its cost would be. Whichever way she presented the argument, pre- or postpetition, the bankruptcy lawyer replied, "That's a good argument."

> ALICE. During the early months after LTV declared bankruptcy, we would go to meetings with LTV retirees at which the level of anger was high. At times I was afraid the tension would erupt into violence. I did not know what to do or say. But as time went on, we knew Ralph would say, "It's time to get out the baseball bats." Some people would cheer and some would laugh. But, in a way, Ralph spoke for all of us: it's time we did something to make a change in the situation. After a time I realized that there were others in Solidarity who reacted as I did when violence against person or property was suggested.
>
> STAUGHTON. How do retirees have any clout, any power? They can't strike. They can't [if they are retired steelworkers] vote for officers of the union. The union will modify their benefits and not put it up to retirees for ratification. You think of these things and you think, this is a powerless group of people. But somehow, we stirred up a storm.
>
> ALICE. I think one thing the retiree movement has indicated is that if you are a retiree, one little voice can't do anything. But I think Solidarity experienced that when one, two, or three busloads of people arrived somewhere, we got a response. I felt, as a lawyer, if I were to call them up or send them a letter and say, "I want to talk to you," do

you think they would take the trouble? No way. But if I come and there are three busloads of people outside, they are going to say, "Alice, won't you come in?" And I say, "Yes, and I'm not going in alone. I'm bringing these people with me." Then we begin to be able to grapple with them.

STAUGHTON. Between the 17th of July, which I believe was a Thursday, and I think it was the second Saturday after that when the first rally took place downtown, Delores informed me that I was going to be her lawyer and she wanted me to be at that rally. I remember that on the day of the rally there was a little article in the Youngstown *Vindicator* which said that at the LTV plant in East Chicago, Indiana, there was a strike connected with the benefits. We were all trying to figure out what was going on. I was convinced that day, and I am convinced sitting here six years later, that some women—like Cora and Jean and Marian—went out and started picketing at the plant because LTV had taken away their medical insurance. I think the security guards roughed up the women or pushed them around and treated them disrespectfully. The whole mill walked out—that's my understanding. And a couple of days later the International said it was an official strike. Ever after the International claimed credit for calling the strike, I don't think they had a thing to do with it. I think it was first of all the women, the wives of retirees, and secondly the guys inside who felt ashamed when they saw how these women were being treated outside the plant.

I remember, at the rally, listening to Congressman Traficant and the Steelworkers union subdistrict director Joe Clark and other speakers. And I thought to myself, that's not going to get results. What's going to get results is the way they did it in Indiana. People just did it themselves. They hit the bricks and brought pressure on the company.

The Retirees' Tale

Cora Sanchez, Jerry Morrison, and Jean Rider became officers of Solidarity USA. None of them had ever done anything like this before.

CORA. I was in bed. I never get up early. I always lie in bed and listen to the Dan Ryan talk show. It came over the air that LTV had gone bankrupt and there was no insurance, no hospitalization. That woke me up real fast!

I ran all over the house looking for my husband, Augie, to tell him. He told me, "Calm down! Calm down, now. It's not true. That's just a rumor." And I said, "What's it on the radio for?"

JERRY. I heard Delores Hrycyk on the radio saying, "We're going to have a rally downtown. Come down." I went down. She started talking. She was mad as hell and she wasn't going to take it anymore. It was just how I felt. And I said to myself, it's time that people get off their duffs and, instead of reading about it and listening about it, start doing something about it. And I just dedicated my life right then and there to doing something about it, seeing what I possibly could do.

I listened to her, and in the crowd there was a guy intermittently coming in with a bullhorn whom I didn't know. It was Ed Mann. We had a few of the hustlers up there talking on the microphone, telling us not to worry. But Ed Mann wasn't like that. And neither was Delores. And I said, now these are the guys I want to be involved with.

CORA. We went to the rally at Federal Plaza. All these big shots got up there and talked and we asked the union man, "What's going to happen to us?" And he said, "You have to wait and see." I'll never forget his words. It made me so mad. I thought, "I'm not going to wait and see. What these people are going to do, I'm going to be right with them." So that's how I got involved with Solidarity.

JEAN. I remember the first meeting we had. My husband stood up and said that he would sign up people to join Solidarity. It wasn't named yet. We divided up into sections. We were from Austintown, so he took Austintown and the West Side.

CORA. When Delores started her group, she told the women to come to these meetings. I'd never been to a meeting. I stayed home and scrubbed and baked cookies. Solidarity has really changed me. I don't do that anymore.

JEAN. My kids tell me, they can't believe all I'm doing. I used to stay home and bake pies and bread and all that stuff.

Petitioning the Court

By early August 1986, LTV, fearing that the East Chicago strike would spread to its other mills, had sought and received permission from the Bankruptcy Court to put retirees back on insurance for six months. But the future looked uncertain. The banks that were LTV's secured creditors appealed the decision. Solidarity USA organized a demonstration in front of the Bankruptcy Court at which they presented a petition addressed to Judge Lifland.

> The undersigned are retirees from LTV Steel, their spouses and supporters.
>
> We are coming directly to you because we feel we have no one to speak for us in your Court. . . . Please consider the following:
>
> 1. *Promised payment of medical expenses, life insurance, and pensions, should be given priority over ordinary business debts.* A business debtor can declare a business loss, go into bankruptcy, etc. A retiree who must regularly take insulin for diabetes, who must go to the hospital for necessary treatment, cannot postpone or avoid expense in the same way. In the Youngstown area, at least one person died following July 17 because he could not arrange for alternative coverage and was afraid to go to the hospital for his heart condition without insurance.
>
> 2. *Post-petition medical, life insurance, and pension payments deserve at least as much consideration as the fees of bankruptcy lawyers.* We understand that medical, life insurance, and pension payments that fall due after July 17 can be given the same priority as payments to bankruptcy lawyers if classified as "administrative expenses." We think it would be unfair to pay lawyers 100 cents on the dollar and to give retirees and their surviving spouses less.
>
> *The company that encouraged us to plan our whole lives around the expectation of a secure retirement should not be permitted to turn its back on us now.* We are not asking for charity. The union, acting on our behalf, bargained for fringe benefits instead of current wages so our retirement could be peaceful and secure. These benefits are therefore deferred compensation, taken in place of current wages. Moreover, many of us as retirees pay part

of the cost of our major medical coverage in monthly out-of-pocket payments deducted from our pension checks.

Getting Organized

There were bake sales and a lot of fundraising activities going on. If you're handling much money, you've got to think about taxes. You've got to think about having not-for-profit incorporation.

> ALICE. Incorporation became a way to redistribute power, because you don't have a corporation with just one person. You have to have three incorporators, and then you have to have a president, a vice president, a secretary, and a treasurer. And that did not take in all of the people who were actually taking leadership, so we set up a steering committee. We had at least twelve people on the steering committee, and it was the steering committee that would meet together and make decisions, or would recommend decisions to the membership meeting, which would make the decisions.
>
> We found that we could get a bus and it would cost so much money. "Shall we take it?" And the members would say yes. And Delores would say, "If there's anybody that doesn't have ten dollars for the bus, tell them to come anyway. We'll have a bake sale and we'll raise the money."
>
> Then the committees were set up. The medical committee, that Cora and Jean worked on, helped people when their insurance wasn't paying. There was one man who would write articles for the newsletter every month giving his perspective on what was going on.
>
> I remember trips to Washington when we would divide up into little teams and we'd each go to certain senators and congressmen. Some of them couldn't figure out what we were talking about. They had no conception: retirees? benefits? It was like, "Are you from the moon?" There was no response.
>
> There were others who were responsive but who said, "You've got to stay within the framework of bankruptcy law. And in bankruptcy law, everybody gives."
>
> There were a few people, like Senator Heinz's aide, who listened to the retirees. He took their medical bills and tried to figure out what the problem was and why they felt such anxiety.

City Council Resolutions

Busloads of Solidarity USA retirees and spouses went with LTV retirees from other groups to city councils in the region during the winter of 1986–1987. They asked the Pittsburgh City Council to support LTV retirees in demanding no compromise or concessions in their medical, life insurance, and pension benefits.

On a cold, wet December 2, 1986, Solidarity USA demonstrators joined a rally in Cleveland, followed by a march to the Cleveland City Council. According to a local union newspaper:

> Many carried signs bearing such messages as "LTV Masters of Deceit," "LTV an Expert Employee Traitor," "Liars, Thieves, Vultures," "LTV Has Stolen Our Dreams," "LTV Screws Retirees," and "Steel Pension, Not Steal Pension."
>
> Delores Hrycyk of Solidarity USA, an organization of LTV pensioners, described July 17 as a day of infamy for every worker in America. She said, "LTV committed fraud that day. They promised us a secure retirement, but we got the shaft." She described LTV's actions as murder since some retirees died because they had no medical benefits.
>
> Chanting, "Justice: we fought for it; we struck for it; we earned it; we won't take anything less," the protesters marched to the Blue Cross Headquarters, where they held a brief rally to protest Blue Cross's recent announcement of higher rates for senior citizens and its inhumane attitude toward the retirees on July 17.
>
> Blue Cross employees met the demonstrators with free coffee and donuts.
>
> SEIU Business Agent Mike Murphy spoke, stating, "If they take away our health care, we need nationalized medicine."
>
> The protesters then marched to City Hall for a giant indoor rally.
>
> Hrycyk said, "We're not here to beg; we're just here to get what we earned. We built the country, paid the taxes, and are paying the pension of every politician in this country. . . . Give us what we bargained for. . . . I don't want to see this American dream destroyed. . . . Workers of this country have to unite, come to the grassroots and say we've had enough and want what's coming to us." She demanded a complete Congressional investigation of LTV's merger and bankruptcy, adding, "They're telling me I'm a creditor. No, they stole my pension money. That's why they wanted these mills—to get my pension money. I'm no creditor, they're thieves."

Emergency Legislation

The first governmental response to the plight of LTV retirees came in the form of temporary emergency legislation passed by Congress in October 1986. The law required a company reorganizing in bankruptcy that had not yet filed a reorganization plan to continue to pay retiree health and life insurance benefits until May 15, 1987.

The emergency legislation was extended several times. In June 1988, Congress passed a retiree benefits protection act known in the Mahoning Valley as the Metzenbaum bill. The new law did not protect pension supplements and, as it turned out, offered little protection to medical and life insurance benefits.

> JEAN. I remember Metzenbaum. He told us, "Don't worry. You won't lose a thing. You will not lose one penny." I remember him saying that at least four times to our face.
>
> CORA. When we had the big rally down at Powers Auditorium in January 1987 . . .
>
> JEAN. And in Washington twice.
>
> CORA. He wasn't going to come to the rally in Youngstown, but we kept after him. He even got up and said he came because it's the squeaky wheel that gets greased.
>
> STAUGHTON. In March 1987, there was a meeting in Washington with Metzenbaum and Traficant. Traficant took the position that you should simply pass a law saying companies have to pay retiree benefits no matter what. Period.
>
> Everybody else explained to us that it was absolutely impossible for that law to pass. We would also have preferred such a law. But there are going to be some companies that actually don't have any money. What were they going to do if we passed that law? We had a choice between fighting the good fight for something that wasn't going to go anywhere, or settling for something that you, Marian and Jack, have found completely useless.
>
> CORA. The union backed Metzenbaum's bill too. When we went to Washington, they almost put me in jail, because I passed out a leaflet supporting the Traficant bill. I made a mistake and gave one to Tony Rainaldi, who is a district director of the Steelworkers.
>
> Rainaldi came along and I gave him a leaflet. Pretty

soon this guy came back and said, "You two better go upstairs to that room." I said, "I'm not going to no room!" He said, "Well, we're going to bring the police." And I said, "Well, make sure you bring enough because there's two old ladies here!" That made them mad.

They got the police and we were told to either leave or we would go to jail. So we just stopped. We put our leaflets away and we stayed. It was in the Shoreham Hotel.

The union had all these papers. The union had this long table. Before the union came in we stole all their papers and we hid them under the table and they had nothing to pass out to us. We took all their badges. We had our pockets full of badges. The union took the microphone down so Solidarity couldn't talk.

MIKE. Now if your kids had done that, you would have whipped their butts.

CORA. Oh, yeah. If we'd have done that, we would have been grounded for a month!

JACK. They got smarter then to make sure nobody gets anything under the Metzenbaum bill.

CORA. But we're trying to get him to amend it because of what happened to you guys at GF especially.

MARIAN. We were stuck because GF had no money. LTV had money. We didn't. Still don't.

CORA. I got threatening phone calls after this. Augie was in Puerto Rico and I was living here by myself. I was scared to death but I said, "You better say or do what you want now, because I don't run scared." Well, I never got a call after that.

MARIAN. You did right to tell them you weren't scared.

CORA. I *was* scared. I kept everybody's telephone number right by the phone.

$26.82

In August 1987, the United Steelworkers of America negotiated a new labor agreement. The agreement provided that early retirees would receive from LTV approximately 90 percent of the pension supplement that had been negotiated for steelworkers forced into early retirement by mill shutdowns. (The supplement was $400 a month for the typical early retiree. Ninety percent came to $360 a month.) In addition, the new agreement provided that all employees and retirees would have to pay $26.82 per month toward the cost of basic hospitalization insurance. Current employees would have the money taken out of a profit-sharing pool, not out of their paychecks. But in the case of retirees, the $26.82 was deducted from their pension checks. If the company made sufficient profit, retirees would be reimbursed in April for the amount they contributed during the previous year.

Retirees received checks in April 1988 reimbursing the $26.82 per month deducted from their pension checks at the end of 1987. But when LTV published its third-quarter report in the fall of 1988, it appeared that LTV was taking advantage of a new accounting rule to wipe profits off their books for 1988. Retirees notified LTV that if they did not receive satisfactory assurances that the $26.82 for 1988 would be returned, Solidarity USA would stage a demonstration outside LTV's headquarters in Cleveland.

A busload of retirees from Retirees Against Greed and Exploitation (RAGE) arrived from Canton, Ohio, to swell the ranks of Solidarity USA demonstrators in front of the LTV Steel building in Cleveland. LTV got the message. Retirees were reimbursed by LTV in April 1989.

PORKY. But there was no interest when we got the $26.82 back.

Confrontation with Blue Cross

For reasons not known to LTV retirees, their major medical insurance coverage was transferred from the Metropolitan Life Insurance Company to Blue Cross Blue Shield of Ohio. Blue Cross was already administering the basic hospitalization coverage, and it continued to do so. LTV was self-insured for the basic hospitalization coverage—that is, LTV paid Blue Cross the amounts paid out in claims plus an administrative fee—but retirees paid the entire cost of the major medical program through premiums deducted from their pension checks.

Soon after Blue Cross took over the major medical, retirees began to notice that claims were not being paid as they had been before. In April 1989, someone reported to the steering committee of Solidarity USA, "Lab work used to be covered while in the hospital. Now they are only paying 80 percent after the deductible." But LTV had said in a letter in December 1989 that there would be no change in benefits.

At the membership meeting in June, Jerry Morrison exclaimed:

Blue Cross Blue Shield is deciding how sick you are and is saying how long you can stay in the hospital. They should expedite payment of medical insurance and pay more of the bills, and not tell doctors what care your insurance will pay for. We're going to go up and protest in front of their building. The last time we went to Cleveland, we got our $325 back [return of $26.82 for twelve months of 1988]!

And at the July meeting, Jerry said, "The dignity of a person is paying his bills."

After some correspondence and phone calls, Blue Cross was notified that Solidarity USA would appear at their Cleveland office on October 18, 1989. In the meantime bills and "explanation of benefits" forms had been collected and numerous examples identified where items previously covered 100 percent by the basic hospitalization program were being paid 80 percent under major medical. Not only did retirees have to pay the premiums for the major medical coverage, but there was a lifetime cap of $50,000 per person as well as an annual cap on major medical benefits.

Blue Cross said that it would not meet with Solidarity USA. Solidarity USA said that it was coming anyway. Blue Cross then said that it would meet with only three representatives; but rather than endure a picket line outside their building, Blue Cross relented and met with the two dozen or so Solidarity USA members who appeared at the designated time. Solidarity's agenda included the following questions and answers:

Why is Blue Cross not paying 100 percent of what used to be paid under the basic plan? How can items that used to be paid 100 percent under the basic policy now be paid 80 percent under major medical? Put what the lifetime limit is and how much of it has been used on each major medical statement. Have a person at the Blue Cross office in Youngstown that people can go to with their papers to get problems resolved or effectively appealed or payment expedited.

A representative of Blue Cross explained that they service what LTV bought. The benefits are set out in the benefits booklet.

A retiree complained about Blue Cross's telephone service: "The 800 number stays busy. You can't get through. An 800 number is not adequate for a person with a stack of papers. We need a person to answer claims problems."

Porky produced papers showing that when he had a stress test in the hospital in 1988, everything was covered; but when he had a stress test in the doctor's office in 1989, they took off the $100 deductible and then paid a percentage under major medical. "What difference does it make whether the test is done in the doctor's office or in a hospital?"

Porky later reported that Blue Cross told his doctor, "If the hospital sent the bill they would pay 100 percent; but if [the test is] done in the hospital but billed by a doctor who has an office in the hospital, they pay 80 percent."

Murph asked, when testing is done as an outpatient and surgery is done as an inpatient, why don't you pay for these tests when it saves money to have the tests done outside the hospital? Solidarity urged that the same rules should apply for everybody, whether or not they are in the hospital.

Cora had her papers showing that an "EKG was covered in one place but not in another. But the LTV letter says no change in coverage." Murph added: "You're being paid to provide the same coverage as Metropolitan."

"We're representing folks who are hurting," said Ed Mann. "I negotiated these [benefits] with the company. We gave up wages." And speaking about bills that "before were not major medical," Ed asked, "why are they major medical now? There is a lifetime cap on major medical benefits."

Two days after the meeting with Blue Cross in Cleveland, Cora told Solidarity that Blue Cross had taken her EKG off major medical and was paying 100 percent under basic. But, she said, "satisfying a few individuals does not take care of thousands of others." At the next meeting of Solidarity USA at the end of October, Cora reported as cochairperson of the medical committee:

> CORA. Blue Cross says, "We are doing what LTV tells us to do." Each [LTV and Blue Cross] puts the blame on the other. Individuals are being taken care of, but are we satisfied? No. We want [the same] for everybody. What they used to pay under basic is now major medical, and there's a limit on major medical. . . . How can two companies use the same book and get different answers?

> JEAN. We just went over to LTV. We had a picket line in front of LTV's Youngstown office about our benefits. Finally they let a group of us go in and we said, "We want these bills settled." There was one man that had $17,000 that hadn't been paid. They were just holding him up. We went in and Bruce Mateer, LTV's benefits man, looked at

each one of these bills with us. After that, whenever we
had any trouble, we went over and saw them.

CORA. At first they were going to let only the people who
had the problems go in and talk. And we said a representative of Solidarity would go in with each one. They said,
"No, we can't do that." So I said, "Then we'll just stay here."
Then they got used to us and they let us bring anybody.
Now, all we have to do is tell people to say, "Solidarity sent
me," or "Cora sent me."

The first time we went to LTV, there were all these
policemen there. I walked in and shook the cop's hand because I grew up with him. That night I got a telephone call
and they said, "Cora, we were told to watch for you and to
arrest you if you misbehaved."

Health Benefit Guaranty Corporation or Universal Health Care?

In the fall of 1988, the Tunnel Rats for Workers Solidarity (a group of LTV
Steel retirees in Aliquippa, Pennsylvania), circulated a petition that said:

> We the People demand that health and pension benefits of active
> workers and retirees of LTV and other companies in bankruptcy
> can not be modified or reduced unless necessary to avoid a com-
> pany's full bankruptcy (Chapter 7).
>
> Since some companies do go fully bankrupt (Chapter 7),
> We the People demand that a Health Benefit Guaranty Corpo-
> ration (HBGC) be established to guarantee transitional health
> care benefits for unemployed workers, and permanent health
> care benefits for retirees of bankrupt companies like LTV.

Solidarity USA lent its support to this proposal, as did RAGE in
Canton, but Solidarity USA did not feel that a Health Benefit Guaranty
Corporation (HBGC) would take care of enough people. The Solidarity USA steering committee debated: if you want to extend government
medical insurance to people who don't have it, who should be included?

The Tunnel Rats' answer was, "Guarantee insurance if you earned it."
As Carole McMahon of the Tunnel Rats put it, "These are people that
earned this health care. They were promised it and they should get it."

But what about the employee who isn't retired and is unemployed,
or works but never had insurance? During a meeting of Solidarity USA
in February 1989, Delores Hrycyk expressed her views:

> I am a firm believer that we need medical care for all. Service
> jobs can't afford it. Some people stay on welfare from generation
> to generation to keep their medical card. That discourages work.
> They never had a chance to earn it. Every man, woman and child
> should have the care they need. Put all the money together—
> Medicare, Medicaid—that route excites me.

A consensus formed within Solidarity USA to endorse the principle
of health care for all, not just for one group, because that expresses solidarity. RAGE concurred. Bob Burns of RAGE told Carole that the HBGC
"doesn't cover enough people. RAGE is for national health care insurance."

Collective Bargaining Demands

In August 1988, Solidarity USA asked the Steelworkers district director
Coyle to come to the September meeting of Solidarity USA and to answer some of the retirees' questions.

> What is going on? What is being done about taxation of [supple-
> ments]? What is the union going to do for retirees? What will
> the union be raising in the next negotiations—specifically, what
> does the union intend to do about the $26.82 charge for basic
> medical insurance? And, especially, how can retirees have input
> into the process of formulating bargaining demands?

The union declined to send a representative to meet with Solidarity
USA. But the September 1988 issue of the Solidarity USA *Newsletter*
carried a list of ten "collective bargaining demands":

> The following bargaining demands for the next round
> of negotiations between LTV and USWA were moved,
> seconded, and approved at the Solidarity USA meeting on
> August 28:
>
> 1. Retirees must have a voice in contract negotiations that
>   vitally affect them. The USWA should offer retiree groups
>   a seat at the negotiating table. . . . After a contract has
>   been negotiated, the USWA should take an advisory poll
>   of retirees before submitting the contract to a ratification
>   vote by active employees.
>
> 2. The $26.82 per month contribution by retirees to the
>   cost of their basic medical coverage should be abolished.
>   When this insurance was negotiated it was supposed to
>   be without charge. LTV has plenty of money to pay what

it promised to pay. Also, with regard to 1988 we want a written accounting as to LTV's ability to refund the $26.82 per month contribution for this year.

3. The pension supplement should be restored to $400. If this is impossible, the Social Security and state income tax deductions on pension supplement payments should be abolished. If these deductions cannot be abolished, the payments themselves should be increased so that the company (not the retiree) pays any taxes of this kind.

Other demands had to do with benefits for surviving spouses, retirees on disability, an automatic cost-of-living increase, and other benefits changes.

These demands were sent to the union. There was no response. In December 1988, a retiree in Indiana Harbor called with information about a meeting of union officials in Florida. He said he was "afraid the union will go to the judge as to what they'll do before going to retirees." Solidarity USA wrote to the president of the union, Lynn Williams, and asked him to permit retirees to attend the meeting of the basic steel industry conference. The union was reached by phone and the message to Solidarity USA was that retirees could not participate, not even as observers.

Meeting with the Union

"The contract is up in 1990," said Jerry Morrison, who had recently become president of Solidarity USA. "They're squeezing us on medical and on the $400. We will go back and fight if we have to." "And not go to Pittsburgh and be docile like before," added Bob Burns. "If we go, we're going in. We built that hall!" responded Jerry, referring to the Steelworkers' headquarters. "We sent letters to Rainaldi and Coyle and Williams [international union officials] and we've had no answer for a year. They act as if we didn't exist," said another voice. Drawing on the tactic that had worked with Blue Cross, the speaker added: "Tell the union we're coming on a certain day."

That certain day when buses rolled into Pittsburgh from Youngstown, Canton, and Aliquippa was December 7, 1989.

During the latter part of November 1989, LTV notified retirees that the premiums for major medical insurance were to be sharply increased. This added fuel to the fire. Cora wrote a report saying that when her husband retired in 1985, the major medical premium for a married couple not yet on Medicare was $41.74 per month; by January 1989, it was $86.66; and it was going to be raised in January 1990 to $141.32, an increase of $54.66.

This is in addition to $26.82 we pay for hospital benefits. This
will raise us to $168.14 a month that they are taking from our
checks for medical benefits, and don't forget the $40.00 we lost
and on top of that we have to pay FICA taxes on our supplement
and then we pay state and federal taxes. Some retirees are getting a little over $300.00 now. How are they going to live?

We were in Cleveland three weeks ago for a meeting with
Blue Cross Blue Shield. They never told us of a raise. It is like a
slap in the face. We are paying more and more and getting less
and less coverage. . . . We have a $50,000 limit on major medical
and for some people they are reaching it. We have to fight to get
universal health care for all. So I guess Solidarity USA hits the
streets again.

Upon arriving at union headquarters in Pittsburgh, retirees were
directed away from media cameras to a room at the nearby Hilton Hotel.
Some went to the Hilton, but others set up a picket line outside Steelworker headquarters. At the Hilton retirees were finally able to voice
their demands to union representatives.

> JERRY. There are no retirees on the union bargaining com-
> mittees. They tell us we're not paying members.

> ANOTHER RETIREE. I'm a steelworker who brought in the
> CIO. I go downtown and ask the union a question. They
> say, "We don't represent retirees."

> ANOTHER RETIREE.Why can't retirees have a say at least as
> to retiree benefits? Why can't we retain our voting rights?
> We are treated like second class citizens. Our retiree
> group has no say. That's not democratic.

The discussion went in several directions before returning to the
question of input from retirees. "I've had experience on the wage policy
committee," said Ed Mann.

> We want input in negotiations and not just as advisers. [If we
> participate and it's a bad deal], we can't put [the blame] on you.
> We want a piece of the action—not to be told, "This is the best
> we can do for you." We don't want to solve our problems one by
> one with LTV. We want to solve them as a union for everyone. . . .
>
> There are people in the union that want us to be adversaries.
> We support young workers. We want to help organize. But when
> we hear that [active workers won't take any more hits] for retirees,

they're splitting us apart.

Before the meeting was over, demonstrators who had been picketing at union headquarters were invited into the hotel room where the meeting with union officials was taking place. Ed Mann spoke again:

> We want to be on a negotiating committee for retirees, not on an advisory committee. . . . There is no one here who is not for the union. If the union goes down, we're dead. We want the right to ratify . . .

Are We Radicals?

Retirees who built the union agonize that the union has lost the vision it used to have. They are brokenhearted lovers.

> PORKY. Years ago, when I was a griever at Truscon, I was always considered a radical even though I was a part of the union. I was a radical because I never agreed with a lot of the things that the local union wanted.
>
> MARIAN. You're not really a radical to me. You're not way out. You're just standing up for your beliefs and trying to get across, and because you do that you're a radical.
>
> JERRY. I can remember the first time I got up. I never got up and made speeches. All these dignitaries were sitting there. "We have a representative here from Solidarity USA. He'd like to say a few words." The minister was there. One politician said, "What do you think they're doing now, Mr. Morrison?" I said, "They're pissing in your face and telling you it's raining." I mean, the crowd roared. "That's it! You're telling it like it is." I talked right to the mill people that were there.
>
> ALICE. I'm reminded of a song that was sung at the memorial service for Ed Mann: "Oh, you ain't done nothing if you ain't been called a Red."
>
> I think there is a question, are you within bounds or are you out-of-bounds. When you stand up and fight for your rights, some people are going to say you are out-of-bounds.
>
> JEAN. This country was started by people who, most people would say, were out-of-bounds.

JACK. The union was too. Don't forget that. The union was started by people who were out-of-bounds.

JEAN. Don't you think that the union has now become like a big corporation? It is not run by ordinary people anymore. You have people running our union that aren't even from our country. Lynn Williams, president of the Steelworkers, can go back to Canada and have his national health care. He doesn't have to worry.

And they don't have conferences in Youngstown. They go to Hawaii or places like that to have their conferences. They don't go first class. They go up-upper class.

Solidarity Unionism

In May 1990 there was a Conference on Workers' Self-Organization in Minneapolis. My friend Stan Weir was to be the keynote speaker. He was unable to come because of the diverticulitis from which he died a few years later. I was asked to substitute.

The gathering was in a large, ramshackle building that must have hosted dozens of similar occasions. I had been immersed in the labor movement in Chicago, northern Indiana, and Youngstown for over twenty years as historian and lawyer. I resolved to "let it all hang out" and gave a long talk. Afterward, David Roediger said I should have it made into a small book called Solidarity Unionism. *Charles H. Kerr was persuaded to help carry out the project, with wonderful drawings by Mike Konopacki.*

The entire booklet is too long to reproduce here but is scheduled to become available from PM Press. Below I offer most of chapter 3, "Is There an Alternative to the Unionism We Have Now?," and three segments from an autobiographical booklet by Ed Mann that appeared in Solidarity Unionism *as an appendix.*

There is no way to prove in advance that there is a realistic alternative to CIO business unionism.

Still, there are some useful things that we can say to each other at this point in time, to help us make the attempt. I will, first, try to pinpoint the essential difference in principle between existing unionism and the unionism some of us are trying to build, and then, show that at various times in the past shopfloor committees and parallel central labor unions like those we are beginning to build have been very effective indeed. . . .

Solidarity Unionism

The essential principle of CIO business unions is verticalism. They are hierarchical organizations. Power flows from the top down: the international union officers appoint the staff men, the district directors depend on the international union for their share of the dues check-off money, the staff men take over the local union grievances after the first couple of steps, the grievance committeemen settle grievances without consulting the members who filed the grievances and who, more than anyone, are affected by how the grievances are settled.

If you like things done this way, you can stop reading right here. You may want to put your energy into electing new officers to run these top-down unions.

But if you *don't* like things done in this way, a moment's thought will lead to the conclusion that the *structure* of hierarchical unions will not change simply by electing new people to run them. You will start looking for alternative kinds of structure.

The essential principle of the alternative kind of unionism that one glimpses in the early 1930s, or in the very small steps that workers in Youngstown have made in the last few years, is solidarity. Alternative unionism is solidarity unionism. It is relying, not on technical expertise, or on numbers of signed-up members, nor yet on bureaucratic chain of command, but on the spark that leaps from person to person, especially in times of common crisis.

A college teacher or a lawyer is likely to experience victory or defeat as a personal matter. Victories are felt to be personal coups. If a big case is lost, or one fails to get tenure, it is believed to be due to some personal act or omission. Similarly, the wins and losses of others are perceived as those others' private business.

Most workers, on the other hand, are forced to recognize that the power of the employer is much greater than that of any single employee, acting alone. The Horatio Alger myth that individual punctuality and application can overcome all obstacles does not correspond with the powerlessness experienced in a mine disaster or a plant shutdown. It follows that the only realistic way to deal with such common problems is to act together.

The words "an injury to one is an injury to all" express this understanding. Above all, this recognition is expressed in the *action* of ordinary rank-and-file workers, when they walk off the job in support of each other, or in other ways take risks for the good of all.

Consider the beginning of Polish Solidarity.

When Anna Walentynowicz was fired from her job as a crane operator, in the Lenin shipyard in Gdansk, Poland, in August 1980, her workmates struck demanding her reinstatement. Other shipyards struck in sympathy. In two days the workers at the Lenin yard had won their demands. Walentynowicz and Lech Walesa were reinstated, and the Polish government promised to build a monument honoring workers killed in the strike of 1970.

The question was posed whether the Lenin yard strikers should stay out on behalf of the demands of other shipyards. As Walentynowicz tells the story:

> Alina Pienkowska and I went running back to the hall to declare a solidarity strike, but the microphones were off. The shipyard loudspeakers were announcing that the strike was over and that everyone had to leave by six P.M. The gates were open, and people were leaving.
>
> So Alina and I went running to the main gate. And I began to appeal to them to declare a solidarity strike, because the only reason that the manager had met our demands was that the other factories were still on strike. I said that if the workers at these other factories were defeated, we wouldn't be safe either. But somebody challenged me. "On whose authority are you declaring this a strike? I'm tired and I want to go home." I too was tired, and I started to cry . . . .
>
> Now, Alina is very small, a tiny person, but full of initiative. She stood up on a barrel and began to appeal to those who were leaving. "We have to help the others with their strikes, because they have helped us. We have to defend them." Somebody from the crowd said, "She's right!" The gate was closed.

The strike that gave birth to Polish Solidarity followed.

At the moment of crisis, Anna Walentynowicz took the position that only if the Lenin workers continued their strike on behalf of the workers at the other shipyards would the Lenin workers be "safe." Clearly she was saying that workers, to preserve their rights, need above all else to preserve their solidarity.

Another example of solidarity comes from Guatemala. In February 1984, the owners of its Coca-Cola plant announced that the enterprise was a failure and closed the plant. According to historian Jack Spence: "The workers immediately occupied the premises. The owners then offered about 6 months severance pay. The workers demanded that the money be used to keep the plant in operation." The owners soon thereafter left the country. The workers addressed their demands to Coca-Cola International. "As days stretched into payless weeks, and weeks into months, about one hundred workers had to drop out. Of the remainder, eighty were organized into work teams to find work to support the families of all. The rest divided into two work teams, each occupying the factory for 24 hour shifts." It took more than a year to find a new owner, and to reopen the plant. But the new owner agreed to hire only 265 of the workers, putting the remaining 85 on a first-hire waiting list. Professor Spence inquired if the 85 who did not go back to work were the workers with least seniority. No, he was told, "eighty-five volunteers stepped forward to place themselves on the waiting list. They had been out of work almost a year."

A last example of solidarity, showing that North American workers can do it just as well as anyone else, is the inspiring story of clerical and technical workers at Yale University. In organizing a union, in negotiating a first contract, Local 34 and its organizers wrote a textbook on solidarity unionism. The union rejected the use of literature for the first year of its drive, and made no efforts to get members to sign union cards for over a year and a half. Instead its organizers, mostly rank-and-file workers, endlessly talked with individuals and small groups.

> When one of the organizers first approached Beverly Lott, "He didn't say, 'Just sign a card.' What he said was, 'I want you to do some work. I want you to help, because it's going to be your union, not my union, because I'm going to be gone some day.'"

All committees were open to any member; the Organizing Committee came to have 450 members. Not only did Local 34 pledge not to collect any initiation fees or dues until a first contract had been secured, it also promised that the members would set their own dues.

The most dramatic expression of solidarity at Yale came from the blue-collar service and maintenance workers in Local 35. They had been organized for years, and clerical workers had regularly crossed their picket lines. Yet when the clerical workers struck for a contract, the members of Local 35 stayed out.

> [T]he administration sent a personal letter to each member of Local 35 threatening disciplinary action against those who failed to come to work. . . . On the evening of October 2, five hundred members of Local 35 assembled at the Methodist Church and marched to President Giamatti's house, where each deposited in a box . . . a small blue card reading, "I'm out. I have a right to be out. I'm staying out. Yale should settle or arbitrate."

Shopfloor Committees

When I speak of a shopfloor or stewards' committee, I mean a committee based in the informal work groups that Stan Weir writes about, made up of elected representatives who continue to work full-time.

Informal work groups, as Stan Weir has described them, come to provide for their members what amounts to a family-on-the-job. "Led by natural on-the-job leaders, they conduct daily guerrilla skirmishes with their employers and often against their official union representatives. These groups are the power base for insurgencies from below." In Youngstown, I have repeatedly dealt with shops where workers felt unserved or abandoned by union leaders, and elected a committee to represent them better. The persons elected to such committees tend to be individuals who have earned the trust of their fellow workers on the shop floor over a period of years.

I also mean a committee that may exist in a nonunion shop, or, where a union has been recognized, may function alongside the official union structure. It is an idea that goes far back in our country's labor history.

David Montgomery, for example, has described how in the era of World War I workers formed elected committees in individual plants to stand up to the employer through direct action. Thus at the Westinghouse plant near Pittsburgh, workers created an "inplant organization made up of their own elected delegates" that cut across traditional craft lines. The permanent presence of this active group representative right there on the shop floor, "all day every day," added something essential to the very different kind of representation that a national union could offer. At Westinghouse, as Montgomery tells the story, workers recruited employees of all descriptions (including clerical workers) into an organization marvelously named the Allegheny Congenial Industrial Union. This organization "copied the IWW by devoting itself to struggles around demands, rather than negotiating contracts, . . . but it also used a system of departmental delegates inside the plant as its basic structure."

The improvised shop committee at Westinghouse in the World War I period may be compared to the shopfloor activities carried on in industries such as steel, auto, rubber, and electrical equipment during the early days of the CIO at a time when unions were not yet exclusive bargaining agents, collective bargaining agreements had not been signed, and, as a result, shop stewards were still free to orchestrate slowdowns and wildcat strikes in support of their constituents' demands.

John Sargent, first president of the CIO union at Inland Steel in East Chicago, Indiana, tells what happened there in the years between the

Little Steel Strike of 1937 and the beginning of World War II in 1941. . . .

The same thing happened during the late 1930s in automobile plants. At the GM plant in Atlanta, one participant recalls:

> Now actually in the signed agreement we didn't get anything except recognition for our members only. We were not permitted to bargain for anyone but our members. But, I think, following the settlement of the strike we had some of the most effective bargaining in the plant that I think we ever had, because of the way we handled it.
>
> The company wanted to bargain with the people individually, so they adopted what they called an open-door policy. The manager's door was always open. Any employee could come in and discuss any problems he had with them at any time. And what we did, in the departments, one employee had a problem, we all had a problem, and we would all go down to the office to discuss our problem with them. Now that shut the whole plant down, because they had to settle the department's problem before they could get the plant to operate.

Such "solidarity unionism," inspired by and permeated with the spirit of solidarity, should be distinguished from a merely tactical use of solidarity.

For example, the AFL-CIO pamphlet, *The Inside Game*, although subtitled *Winning with Workplace Strategies*, presents a tactical rather than a strategic or principled argument for solidarity.

The booklet begins promisingly. In situations where a strike would be ineffective, it suggests, "staying on the job and working from the inside may be more appropriate and effective." What does this mean? *The Inside Game* explains:

> Increasingly, unions are finding they must actually go back in time to find ways to cope with the refusal of employers to bargain in a fair and equitable manner.
>
> Back to a time when there was no National Labor Relations Act, no public employee collective bargaining laws.
>
> Back to a time when the only rule was that *there were no rules* and workers had only their numbers, their solidarity and their aggressive collective actions to protect their jobs and pry contracts from employers.

The Inside Game goes on to say that one of the names unions have given to these techniques is simply "building solidarity."

Case studies at the end of *The Inside Game* include provocative specific ideas, such as:

1. When the contract runs out, go on working and ask members to pay union dues voluntarily;

2. "Work to rule" by refusing to work outside job descriptions or to work overtime;

3. Sit-downs in such large numbers that the employer will hesitate to fire or arrest all those involved;

4. Holding regular meetings on the shop floor as well as at the union hall;

5. Setting up a voluntary "Solidarity Fund" to assist fellow workers fired or disciplined;

6. Mass presentation of grievances, by workers who leave their work stations and go to management offices to complain;

7. Expanding the number of stewards to include more people holding key jobs in the plant;

8. Boycotting company Christmas parties, banquets and dinners;

9. Taking over in-plant meetings called by the company;

10. "[S]inging solidarity songs in the employee cafeteria just below the executive offices."

These are indeed the sorts of actions by means of which rank-and-file workers built CIO unions in the 1930s. But do the authors of *The Inside Game* intend that this "building solidarity" style of action become a way of life? Do they, for example, seek to institutionalize the abolition of the dues check-off, or direct action on the shop floor, or a shop steward for every foreman?

Not on your life! The object of solidarity tactics is said by *The Inside Game* to be convincing the employer "that a decent contract is in management's own self-interest": that is, by convincing the employer that conventional bargaining, in which the employer can deal with full-time representatives who in turn act as policemen of their own rank and file, is preferable to rank-and-file mass action.

This is exactly what John L. Lewis did fifty years ago, when the CIO was organized. He used the radical direct action of the sit-down at Flint,

Michigan, in January–February 1937 to frighten Myron Taylor of U.S. Steel into recognizing the Steel Workers Organizing Committee in March 1937. Once the CIO unions had been recognized as responsible bargaining partners with whom management could negotiate "a decent contract . . . in management's own self-interest," Lewis got rid of the radicals who built the CIO.

The critical analytical error of *The Inside Game*, as in the general thinking of established unions about their current crisis, is the assumption that labor and management have the same or mutually consistent interests. The dominant organizations in the American labor movement for the past century have made this assumption. It is the assumption that underlies business unionism, because it induces trade unions to leave investment decisions to management while directing their own attention to wages, hours, and working conditions, and to surrender the right to strike (for the duration of collective bargaining agreements) in the belief that workers no longer need the strike to protect their day-to-day interests.

Parallel Central Labor Bodies

Equally deep-rooted in the labor history of the United States is another kind of committee, the council in which the local unions or rank-and-file groups from different places of work in a locality make contact with each other, broaden one another's consciousness, and take common action.

The official AFL-CIO central labor body purports to be such an entity, and there are situations in which it will actually function as such. In other circumstances, workers will have to organize new entities—parallel central labor bodies like the Workers' Solidarity Club of Youngstown—to perform this function.

David Montgomery tells how at the same Westinghouse plant described earlier, a key organizer was dismissed. Two thousand men and women walked out. By the next morning, 13,000 striking workers linked hands to form a huge human chain around the Westinghouse complex. Giant processions of strikers and supporters gradually closed down the whole Monongahela Valley. On November 1, 1916, a parade bedecked with red flags and led by a Lithuanian band invaded steel mills, chain works, and machinery companies, bringing out 36,000 workers. "The ethnic antagonisms that have absorbed the attention of most historians studying the region's workers seemed to melt away, as the angry and joyous tide of humanity poured through the streets."

Essentially the same thing happened in the local general strikes in Minneapolis, Toledo, and San Francisco in 1934. And by whatever name—"district assemblies" in the era of the Knights of Labor, or IWW "mixed locals," or "soviets" in the Russian Revolutions of 1905 and 1917, or local branches of Polish Solidarity—the bodies that coordinate such actions rely not so much on the national organization of all workers in a given craft or industry as on the solidarity of all workers in a particular place.

Again the 1930s prove to be a storehouse of alternatives, as the Los Angeles Labor Networking Committee indicates in its position paper, "The Failure of Business Unionism and the Emergence of a Rank-and-File Alternative." The paper gives the following examples of "history to be retrieved."

> Out of a sitdown strike in the Hormel plant at Austin, Minnesota, in 1933 emerged the Independent Union of All Workers (IUAW). It contained meatpacking workers, grocery clerks, butchers, waitresses, bartenders, and many more. All who were employed . . . could join. Like most rank-and-file organizing efforts at that time, the IUAW was deeply rooted in both workplaces and the general community. It made substantial headway in south-central Minnesota. . . . [T]he IUAW affiliated with the CIO as soon as the new federation came out of the AFL. Representatives of CIO President John L. Lewis immediately split the IUAW into several parts and redistributed them into different international union organizing committees. (How valuable an IUAW-type structure would have been to local P-9 forty-two years later when its 4,000 members were individually forced to take permanent wage cuts in order to loan Hormel the money to build an automated plant nearby which eliminated over 2,500 jobs.)

> [Similarly,] the Maritime Federation of the Pacific (MFP) was formed out of the general Pacific Coast maritime strike of 1934 by separate unions of longshoremen, deckhands, ship's engine room workers, waiters, cooks and stewards, radio operators, mates and engineers. Each grouping had a specific union to concentrate on problems affecting their particular jobs, but all together could move against the employers as a single unit whenever necessary.

> The MFP formalized this waterfront community alliance. In San Francisco the four largest participating unions—the International Longshoremen and Warehousemen; Sailors Union of the Pacific; Marine Firemen, Oilers, Watertenders and Wipers; and the Marine Cooks and Stewards—all had their hiring halls, offices and meeting halls in the Alaska Fishermen's Union Building, a

half block off the Embarcadero, just north of Market Street. The always present antagonisms of the labor market were daily minimized by the friendships struck in the nearby bars and cafes.

The breakdown of the MFP and its parallel on the Gulf Coast occurred . . . because the rank-and-file approach did not conform to that of important AFL officials, including those who would soon form the CIO.

We are not speaking of some organizational chart that anyone will impose on the wonderful variety of workers' self-organization. The point is just the reverse: that these two kinds of committees—the committee formed at the individual workplace, with its elected delegates or stewards, and the committee of all kinds of workers in a given locality—recur and recur whenever working people organize for themselves, without somebody telling them what to do or how to do it.

The committee of all workers in a given locality, or as I have called it, the parallel central labor union, has historically also been the place where independent labor politics got its start. It is easy to see why. When workers of many different lines of work get together, they will naturally talk about and act on problems that affect *all* of them. Often solution of such problems requires political action. For example, in Lowell, Massachusetts during the late nineteenth century, or in Aliquippa, Pennsylvania, and elsewhere in the 1930s, strikes were broken by repressive police chiefs. Workers responded by nominating and electing police chiefs prepared to protect the rights of the people.

At the turn of the [twentieth] century, and in the 1930s, too, local labor parties also campaigned for public ownership and operation of enterprises such as electric power, housing, and factories that their capitalist owners no longer wished to operate. In this sense, local labor parties have typically espoused what can fairly be called a socialist platform. . . .

Summary

In describing new organizational forms—shopfloor committees, parallel central labor unions, nationally funded programs administered by local bodies made up of workers and consumers—I am anxious not to be understood mechanically or over-literally. Labels are not important. The art of this new kind of organizing is to discern where solidarity unionism is beginning to happen, and to help it shape and sustain itself.

We must be ready to recognize new forms in many guises. For instance, in Youngstown, Solidarity USA is a parallel central labor body for retirees, and WATCH [Workers Against Toxic Chemical Hazards] is a central labor body for disabled workers. Thus there can be more than one alternative central labor body: there can be different entities, responding to specific constituencies or problems, but with the common feature of cutting across workplace boundaries. Solidarity USA and WATCH recognize their kinship, meet in the same hall, and fraternally (and sororally) support each other.

Although the forms described are essentially local, in times of crisis shopfloor committees and parallel central labor bodies will reach out to make contact with their counterparts elsewhere. Polish Solidarity is a classic example. Another is the network of miners' committees in the Soviet Union, set up entirely outside the official trade unions, that succeeded in staging a nationwide strike in that immense country. Longshoremen in Spain, meatpackers and coal miners in the United States, have formed the same kind of networks in recent years. We don't need more proof of this phenomenon to know that it can happen.

Appendix: Extracts from We Are the Union by Ed Mann

I Believe in Direct Action

I think we've got too much contract. You hate to be the guy who talks about the good old days, but I think the IWW had a darn good idea when they said, "Well, we'll settle these things as they arise."

I believe in direct action. Once a problem is put on paper and gets into the grievance procedure, you might as well kiss that paper goodbye. When the corporations started recognizing unions, they saw this. They co-opted the unions with the grievance procedure and the dues checkoff. They quit dealing with the rank and file and started dealing with people who wanted to be bosses like them, the union bosses.

We were the troublemakers. We'd have a wildcat strike. The international would say, "Either you get back to work or you're fired." It wasn't the company saying this. It was the union.

The Dolomite Gun and the Bonus System

One strike we led, they had a dolomite gun they used to spray the furnaces after the heat was tapped out. Prior to them getting this piece of equipment we used to have to shovel in the dolomite. It was in the summertime, and the superintendent wouldn't use the gun. It was real hot. So we just stayed on the floor or went to the office and said, "We're not going to do any shoveling until you put that gun on the floor to give us some relief." We got help like that. Most of the superintendents in that time had to come up through the ranks and they knew the conditions of the job. They knew you weren't kidding.

But in a production department, say like where Archie Nelson was where people were scarfing, if they slowed down it affected production. Sometimes the stuff was needed at the next point of operations on a certain timetable. The further a piece of metal gets down through the operation, the more costly it becomes. So the further down the line you make your move or your action, it becomes more costly to the company. If you're at the finish where they are going to ship the pipe and you refuse to load it, because it's gone through all these steps that piece of pipe is worth X number of dollars where when it was in the furnace as molten metal it was worth only pennies.

In the Open Hearth, you worked on a big furnace that held two hundred tons of molten metal. If you slowed down the operation, you'd burn the furnace up. The furnace would melt. And then you had a lot of physical hard work repairing the furnace, shoveling and so on: back-breaking work. The idea was to get the heat out as quick as you could; make your steel; get it out of the furnace so it wouldn't tear the furnace up and you made a little bit of bonus.

The people who could slow down the procedure were the people who charged the furnaces, who put in the scrap and molten iron. These were the charging machine men and cranemen. They had a little control over how the operation went. If your first helper wanted two boxes of raw lime and a box of ore in the furnace to make the steel up to specifications, the charging machine man could give them a little extra or not enough and screw up everything.

The longer you keep molten steel in a furnace the more likely you are to tear up the production equipment. You tap the steel into a ladle. You got to get it out of that ladle and into the molds or it's going to freeze up on the ladle. We're talking about 200 tons of steel in one big chunk. There's the labor of putting new brick in and of the boilermaker doing patchwork. And if you don't get the steel to the blooming mill in a certain period of time it's going to get too cold and they will have to reheat it, which costs money, and it will change the makeup of the steel. You got to hit them where it hurts.

Once they were going to change the bonus system. They were going to give the first helper and the second helper an increase in bonus and cut the third helpers. In other words, they were just moving the money around. Third helpers refused to go out on the job. Second helpers stuck with them. Then there was nobody out there to help the first helpers so they agreed to go out with us. It was a wildcat.

Well, we were out that night. The midnight turn comes out and finds out about this. We are all sitting in the washroom. The company comes out with the president of the local, Danny Thomas.

"What's the problem here?" There's the plant manager and the local union president and so on.

I'm sitting there. As spokesman for the group I said, "They're cutting our bonus. We don't want to hear it."

Danny Thomas says to the superintendent, "You get rid of that guy and your troubles are over." And the whole Open Hearth gang is sitting there. This doesn't hurt me politically at all. It got the guys hotter. They didn't care about getting rid of me. They didn't want to lose our bonus!

The superintendent was crying, "What am I going to do with this steel?"

I said, "Tap it out on the ground. I don't care what you do with it."

He said, "The blast furnace is ready to tap. We got to move that iron."

"Dump it on the ground," I said. "We want our bonus."

They agreed.

"Now who's going to get paid? Are we going to get paid for the time we've been docked here?"

"Oh, we can't do that. You guys didn't do any work."

We said, "The furnace did the work. We want paid or we're going home right now." And it worked.

You wonder why Danny Thomas and I didn't get along? He tells the superintendent that if he gets rid of me his troubles are over.

The Wildcat over Tony's Death

This was the first experience I had that showed that *people* can really be involved. At the time I was Recording Secretary of the local, and John [Barbero] and I were both stewards in the Open Hearth. We filed a grievance with the superintendent about 33 different safety violations. One of the items was we wanted vehicles to have back-up signals. They used big heavy trucks in the pit. There was a lot of noise. It was hard to hear. We wanted a warning horn on the back so when a truck was going to back up the people working there could hear it.

The company rejected the grievance out of hand. They weren't going to discuss any of the 33 demands.

Shortly after the grievance was rejected, a man who was going to retire in about seven days was run over by one of these trucks. He was crushed. He was a well-liked person who had worked there a long time and was about to retire. This happened on day turn, about one o'clock in the afternoon.

I was working afternoon turn that day, three to eleven. I came out to work and somebody said, "Tony got killed."

"How did he get killed?"

"You remember that grievance you filed asking for back-up signals on the truck? The truck backed over him and crushed him."

So I got up on the bench in the washroom and I say to the guys coming to work, "What are we going to do about this? Are we going to work under these lousy conditions? Who's next? Who's going to get killed next? Don't we give a damn about Tony?" The guys agreed to go out.

Now some didn't agree to go out. "What's the matter with you guys? Here you are. A union brother murdered. We had a grievance in and it was rejected. Are you going to let the company pull this shit?"

We actually had to drag some people out because we had all kinds of people. "That's not my problem. I don't work down there. I run a crane."

"Let's get out! Let's go!"

We went up to the union hall. We were the afternoon turn that was supposed to go to work. Day turn was finished working, they've tapped the heats out, and the people working the day turn now come up to the union hall. We've got two turns there. We tell them the situation. They agree, "Shut her down!" The guys called their buddies on the midnight turn from the union hall. "Don't come out to work tonight."

John was out of town that weekend. They were looking to me for leadership. I said, "Here's what we'll do. Rather than get the stewards fired, let's appoint a committee for each area and let's start listing our demands on safety," bypassing the union structure. It worked. Every area—pit, cranes, floor—was represented.

In the meantime Lefty DeLarco, who was departmental chairman of the open hearth at that time, was working day turn. He calls over to the union hall on the company phone and says, "Hey Ed, what's going on? Why aren't these guys coming to work?"

I'm sure the phone is bugged. I could have been fired for leading the strike. I say, "Why don't you come up here, Lefty, and find out?"

The company called the international union rep. "What's going on here?"

"There's nothing going on until these grievances are resolved."

"What grievances?"

We didn't just say, "Goddamn it, Tony got killed and we're shutting it down." We said, "This is what we want. Get a meeting with the company. We'll meet at any time they want."

They set up a meeting for that night, about nine o'clock. They had to get the plant manager from wherever he was. The company said, "We're only going to deal with the departmental chairmen."

I said, "Then you're not going to deal with anybody, because this is the committee." I said, "The only reason you want to deal with Lefty is you want to fire him," which wasn't the case, but it got Lefty off the hook. He wouldn't have to tell the people to go back to work.

We refused even to have the superintendent in the office because it was he who rejected the grievance. We said, "We're not going to deal with him if he can't answer. We want to talk to somebody that has more authority." They brought in the division manager. We met late in the night with the company and all the next day.

They agreed to everything. They wanted this committee to meet with the company on a regular basis on safety conditions, bypassing the safety committee because this was an immediate issue, whereas the safety committee worked on things month by month—a meeting this month to correct a light bulb burned out, next month they come back and say, we don't have any light bulbs.

So next day we have a meeting at the union hall to explain what happened, what we gained, and all that. We're discussing whether we're going back to work or not, and I'm saying to the guys, "Look, if there's anything else you want, let's hear it."

Then the Youngstown newspaper comes out. It reports the accident and the strike and it says, "Tony got killed because of his own negligence." The company sent out that statement.

The guys got furious. "We want that statement retracted in tomorrow's paper." Not just a phone call or a letter. They wanted it in the paper, retracted. The paper doesn't come out for another 24 hours. The guys stayed out another day. And in the next day's paper they retracted that statement and the guys went back to work.

They reprimanded everybody in the Open Hearth that went out, and they gave me three days off. We said, "Wait a minute, take the reprimands away." And they did take them off everybody else. I said, "Hey, I don't care. You guys go back to work."

Other departments didn't go out in sympathy, but there was just no work for them. We made the steel. Everything cost, measured as trainloads of material coming in or scrap half loaded. That's a feeling of power. And it isn't something you're doing as an individual. You're doing it as a group.

If you're not going to *do* something, then you're not going to be a leader, are you? I had credibility. I'd just gotten elected Recording Secretary. I got more votes out of the Open Hearth than the president got. The grievance was rejected. The guy was going to retire. It was an emotional issue. He was a guy everybody liked. It wasn't prepared timing. It fell into place. You've got to recognize those situations. Be there when there are credible steps to take. Some people, it never happens in their lives. I was lucky.

"We Are All Leaders"
The Alternative Unionism
of the Early 1930s

In 1996 Alice and I retired from Northeast Ohio Legal Services and turned our attention to the several nearby prisons then being substituted for shut-down steel mills.

That same year, the University of Illinois published as a volume in its series The Working Class in American History a collection of essays titled "We Are All Leaders": The Alternative Unionism of the Early Thirties. The essays were in the same vein as my own earlier essay on the possibility of radicalism in steel, which appears above.

My introduction to that book represents my most recent, maximally scholarly, fully footnoted statement of what I have come to conclude about the decline of CIO trade unionism. I have corrected one or two minor misstatements of fact. In what follows, references to essays appearing "herein" have to do with essays in the volume to which this piece was the introduction, whereas references to essays "above" have to with portions of the present volume.

When I was growing up, the CIO was considered the most progressive social force in the United States. There were books in our home about the CIO with such titles as *Labor on the March*. My mother belonged to the executive board of the New York City teachers' union. The first picket line I ever joined was at the General Motors offices in New York City during the 1946 United Automobile Workers (UAW) strike. I remember the happiness in my father's face and voice when he came home after speaking to a UAW educational conference in Milwaukee. He had advocated a labor party. After the speech was delivered, reports of it "circulated through the union with the result" that it was published as a UAW pamphlet.[1]

Even then it was evident that the officers of CIO unions were "new men of power." But centralized national unions were said to be necessary because the corporations with which they struggled were organized nationally and produced goods for national markets.[2] Today corporations have reorganized as *multinationals* and compete in the *international* marketplace. These corporations close plants in the United States and move production overseas at will. National AFL-CIO unions watch helplessly, just as national AFL unions looked on helplessly during the Great Depression. Like the national AFL unions of that period, national AFL-CIO unions today not only are hierarchical and bureaucratic structures, out of touch with the concerns of the rank and file, but also do not perform effectively the protective tasks that might justify their existence. The hopes of men and women who built new industrial unions in the 1930s have been disappointed.

It is very difficult to know what was or was not possible in the past. Most of those who took part in the struggles of the 1930s and had a feel for the possibilities and limitations of that time are dead. What one can say with confidence is that the end product of the process, AFL-CIO business unionism, does not meet the needs of working people at the end of the twentieth century. A qualitatively different unionism is needed.

The essays in this book describe a kind of union qualitatively different from the bureaucratic business unions that came to make up the CIO. We are not speculating about "might-have-beens."[3] We direct attention to facts that have been disregarded.

Recent studies of the labor movement of the 1930s in such communities as Flint, Akron, Chicago, Memphis, and Woonsocket, Rhode Island, offer evidence of an alternative unionism that preceded the CIO. What is lacking in many of these studies is an openness to the possibility that history could have been different. For example, Gary Gerstle, after richly chronicling the success of the Independent Textile Union in Woonsocket, nonetheless concludes, "The only realistic, programmatic option for a radical . . . in 1930s Woonsocket involved . . . building the CIO, and extending the New Deal."[4] But Michael Honey is right in stating that the movement for industrial unionism in the 1930s was much larger than the CIO. In Memphis the most important industrial union organizer was a black business agent for an AFL "federal union" (a local union directly affiliated with the national AFL).[5]

We believe that what happened in communities like Woonsocket and Barberton, Ohio, in the 1930s and beyond represents an alternative to the course followed by the mainstream labor movement. To encounter this alternative, one must be prepared to lay aside the notion that the real labor movement, the labor movement that mattered, began with the formation of the CIO in 1935. One must view the 1930s from the perspective of rank-and-file workers who were active in 1932, 1933, and 1934. Our essays tell the story of what such workers did on their own behalf before the formation of the CIO and, in some cases, continued to do for years and even decades thereafter.

What Is "Alternative Unionism"?

The unionism described in these essays has been called "community-based unionism" or "solidarity unionism." Elizabeth Faue says community-based unionism "emphasized local autonomy and community-level organization" and "opposed bureaucratic unionism."[6] By whatever name, this alternative unionism was democratic, deeply rooted in mutual aid among workers in different crafts and work sites, and politically independent. The key to the value system of alternative unionism was its egalitarianism. The seniority system later negotiated by CIO unions caused some workers to lose their livelihood in a layoff, while others continued to work full-time. In contrast, the Independent Textile Union in Woonsocket, the first industrial unions in rubber, and the anthracite workers of eastern Pennsylvania in the 1930s all favored schemes to share or "equalize" the work among all workers who had completed the probationary period, regardless of seniority.[7] The same attitude was evident in the response of the new, independent local industrial unions in Barberton to the Roosevelt recession of 1937–38. According to John Borsos, until the work available dropped below a certain number of hours (typically twenty-four hours a week), Barberton unions insisted that it be equally shared.[8]

The organizational forms of alternative unionism included federal labor unions, ad hoc factory committees, and improvised central labor bodies.[9] Historians have supposed that the general strikes in Toledo, Minneapolis, and San Francisco in 1934 were isolated events. We suggest that, on the contrary, these local general strikes were characteristic of what Rosemary Feurer and Gary Gerstle call the "mobilization" of working-class communities.[10] In the absence of effective national organizations from which they could seek help, rank and filers were obliged to turn to each other and create horizontal networks that in turn generated a distinctive organizational culture and set of attitudes.

Numerically, the self-organization of the rank and file in the early 1930s was at least as effective as the top-down efforts of the CIO a few years later. I have found that this was the case in steel.[11] The picture was similar in other industries. By June 1935 there were a hundred federal labor unions in Summit County, Ohio (including the city of Akron), with 60,000 members.[12] In Flint the citywide council of federal labor unions said it had 42,000 members in March 1934, and AFL records indicate that there were 14,000 members who paid dues. These numbers were roughly equivalent to the 25,000 members claimed by the organizer Bob Travis immediately after the Flint sit-down strike of 1937.[13] Similarly, the United Textile Workers Union witnessed an extraordinary increase in southern membership, from only a few thousand in July 1933 to between 85,000 and 135,000 (a third to a half of the southern textile labor force) a year later.[14]

A Wobbly Resemblance

As this book has come together, I have been struck by the resemblance between the "alternative unionism" of the 1930s and the rank-and-file militancy of the Industrial Workers of the World (the IWW). The following evidence, for the most part unknown to me before this project began, supports that impression.

In the anthracite coal fields, IWW membership from 1906 to 1916 rivaled that of the United Mine Workers (UMW). Perhaps as a result, Michael Kozura points out, "anthracite miners continued to rely on illegal wildcat strikes and other forms of direct action, refused on principle to submit grievances to arbitration, tenaciously resisted the contractual regulation of their labor, opposed union dues check-off, habitually rebelled against the UMW's dictatorial leadership, and sustained this militant syndicalism into the late 1940s."[15]

Individual Wobblies or former Wobblies were often involved in the local industrial unions of the 1930s. Len DeCaux wrote of his fellow CIO militants that "when the CIO lefts let down their hair, it seemed that only the youngest had no background of Wobbly associations."[16] Specific examples abound. Tom Klasey, who helped organize AFL members at Chevrolet in Flint, had been an IWW activist in the Pacific Northwest during World War I. In Austin, Minnesota, organization of the Independent Union of All Workers (IUAW) was led by Frank Ellis, who was "a Wobbly and had taken part in the Wobbly free speech fights out in Everett, Washington," and the IUAW itself was remembered by a contemporary as "the old Wobbly, the old IWW's local." Blackie and Chips, the "1934 men" who taught Stan Weir the history of the San Francisco general strike, were among the many older seamen who paid dues to the IWW until 1936. John W. Anderson jumped up on a car fender to become the chairperson of the 1933 Briggs strike in Detroit, worked as a volunteer IWW organizer for three years, and later became a dissident local union president in the UAW. Freeman Thompson, who joined the National Miners Union in the early 1930s and objected when asked to join the United Mine Workers a few years later, "seemed to have some IWW experience in his background."[17]

A Wobbly style of organizing was sometimes evident even when flesh-and-blood Wobblies were not. David Montgomery has suggested that "in many ways the struggles of 1916–1922 . . . presaged those of at least the early 1930s, that is, before the founding of the Committee for Industrial Organization and the enactment of the Wagner Act."[18] The Westinghouse plant east of Pittsburgh is an example of such continuity. Montgomery describes how just before World War I the Westinghouse workers created an in-plant organization that "devoted itself to struggles around demands, rather than negotiating contracts."[19] More than twenty years later, when the CIO established itself in the same plant, bargaining was at first carried on in the same Wobbly manner. According to Ronald Schatz:

> An arrangement existed whereby plant managers would meet with the leaders of UE Local 601 to negotiate about such issues as hours of work or layoff policy, then depart to post the results of their discussions as if management had merely consulted with the union leadership. Although there were few if any Wobblies . . . in the plant, the local had arrived at an IWW-style bargaining relationship. There were no contracts; all agreements could be abrogated by either party at any time; and grievances were settled quickly according to the strength of the workers on the floor of the plant.[20]

As at Westinghouse, the spirit of alternative unionism often carried over into the strongest *local* unions of the emerging CIO. Many CIO unions, not just in anthracite mining and electrical work but also in the automobile, rubber, and steel industries, initially *opposed* "workplace contractualism" in the form of the dues check-off and written contracts.[21] Sylvia Woods, who belonged to a UAW local in Chicago during World War II, recalled, "We never had check-off. We didn't want it."[22] In rubber, sit-downs at General Tire, Firestone, and elsewhere convinced workers that "progress did not have to await a formal contract."[23] Goodrich Local

5 in Akron, whose 13,000 members made it the largest local union in
the United Rubber Workers, for several years in the 1930s deliberately declined to enter into a collective bargaining agreement.[24] Similarly,
John Sargent recalled the years without a contract at Inland Steel as the
union's best years in winning wages and benefits for its members.[25]

The sit-down strikes in Akron and Flint, far from being planned by
the national CIO, arose spontaneously from below and were initially opposed by CIO leaders. David Brody writes, "President Sherman Dalrym-
ple of the Rubber Workers at first opposed the sit-downs. Spontaneous
sit-downs within the plants accounted for the initial victories in auto
and rubber."[26] Ronald Edsforth confirms that the Flint strike "caught the
U.A.W. hierarchy by surprise. They had not planned any action until the
first of the year." Although CIO and UAW leaders supported the Flint
sit-down once it was under way, their difference with the rank and file
over timing was also a disagreement about the authority to start strikes.
"It seems to be a custome [sic] for anybody or any group to call a strike at
will," Adolf Germer, the CIO representative, complained to John Brophy,
the CIO representative, in November 1936.[27] Louis Adamic investigated
the sit-downs soon after they occurred and concluded that

> many of the rank-and-file automobile and rubber workers,
> as well as many of the organizers in the field and some of the
> organizers in the offices of the rubber and automobile unions,
> thought the world of the sitdown when I asked them about it.
> The top leadership of these unions, however, like the responsible
> leaders of the C.I.O., seemed to view it with misgivings. Some
> did not know what to think of the "damned thing," as an Akron
> leader called it. None went so far as to fight it, but to some of
> them it looked like "dangerous business" in the long run even if
> now it helped to organize unions. They at once liked and feared
> it. Some feared it, perhaps, because it deprived the regular la-
> bor official of much of his authority; others because the sitdown
> was too spontaneous and seemingly haphazard. Too anarchic. It
> threatened to play the devil with the collective bargaining idea.[28]

I emphasize that I am talking about the *character* of the alternative
unionism of the 1930s, not its *causation*. In many communities, such as
the southern textile towns Janet Irons describes, the alternative unionism of the early 1930s developed free of any apparent influence from
IWW or other radicals. In some situations, such as the St. Louis nutpickers' strike, the Southern Tenant Farmers' Union or the first sit-down
in the Alabama steel industry, Communists, Trotskyists, Socialists, or

Musteites played the role that Wobblies did elsewhere.[29] Much more research would be needed to support any general theory of causation. An essentially localized movement that took form more or less simultaneously in literally dozens of communities is unlikely to show any single dominant pattern of cause and effect.

I think it is clear, however, that a community-based, horizontally bonded "culture of struggle," with roots in such epic battles as the 1916 Westinghouse strike, the Lawrence, Massachusetts, strikes of 1912 and 1919, and community-based strikes in coal mining and cotton textile towns during the 1920s,[30] also pervaded the alternative unionism of the early 1930s and the first years of many CIO local unions.

Because of the affinity between the character of the alternative unions we have uncovered and the tradition of the IWW, we have chosen as a title the words embattled workers in both settings used. When Wobblies approached Everett, Washington, on the steamer *Verona* in November 1916, Walker Smith reported, "Sheriff McRae called out to them: 'Who is your leader?' Immediate and unmistakable was the answer from every I.W.W.: 'We are all leaders.'"[31] Likewise on March 7, 1932, about 3,000 unemployed Ford workers tried to march from Detroit to Ford headquarters in Dearborn, and at the Dearborn city limits, about fifty Dearborn police and private police from the Ford plant blocked the road. "'Who are your leaders?' an officer called out. 'We are all leaders!' someone shouted back."[32] After these words were spoken, the authorities in each situation opened fire, killing five men in Everett and four in Dearborn.

Alternative Unionism and the CIO

There appear to be three basic ways of looking at the CIO in relation to the alternative unionism of the early 1930s.

The first view is that at the outset of large social movements there is often a period of mass enthusiasm, egalitarianism, and "primitive democracy" (the phrase was coined by Sidney and Beatrice Webb), but as the movement grows and settles down to its serious tasks, an efficient centralized bureaucracy inevitably takes over. In this view the bureaucratized business union movement that the CIO had become by 1950 was natural and inevitable.

A second interpretation of the CIO in its relation to alternative unionism is that everything depends on the ideology of the leadership. Had Communist leadership been able to survive, it is argued, the CIO might have been very different. This way of looking at things tends to lead to campaigns to replace the top personnel of existing AFL-CIO national unions.

While the authors of these essays naturally differ somewhat among themselves, they lean toward a third way of viewing the 1930s. We propose that the CIO *from the beginning* intended a top-down, so-called responsible unionism that would prevent strikes and control the rank and file. It is true that CIO leaders could not get employers to the bargaining table with merely verbal persuasion. For this reason, they were forced to turn the ranks loose against the corporations. Their ultimate objective, however, was succinctly expressed by John L. Lewis, who in effect told the Senate committee sponsoring the Wagner Act, "Allow the workers to organize, establish strong governmental machinery for dealing with labor questions, and industrial peace will result."[33]

Ronald Radosh characterizes Lewis's motivation similarly: "The 'dangerous state of affairs' [of 1935] might very well have led to 'class consciousness' and 'revolution as well.' Lewis hoped that it could 'be avoided,' and he pledged that his own industrial union was 'doing everything in their power to make the system work and thereby avoid it.'"[34] David Brody also writes about Lewis's interest in taming the new local industrial unions of 1933–35:

> Much of Lewis's sense of urgency in 1935 sprang from his awareness of the pressure mounting in industrial ranks. A local auto union leader told Lewis in May 1935 of talk about craft unions taking skilled men from the federal unions. "We say like h--- they will and if it is ever ordered and enforced there will be one more independent union." Threats of this kind, Lewis knew, would surely become actions under existing AFL policy, and, as he warned the Executive Council, then "we are facing the merger of these independent unions in some form of national organization." That prophecy, Lewis was determined, should come to pass under his control.[35]

Brody rightly stresses that a CIO led by Lewis, a lifelong Republican who "made no bones about his contempt for democratic processes that he considered injurious to the efficient operation of the union as a 'business proposition,'" was likely to display "a remarkable opportunism. . . . With John L. Lewis as the heroic figure of the 1930s, it is not any wonder that those great days did not transform American trade unionism into a social movement."[36]

Many observers on the scene at the time the Wagner Act was passed predicted with essential accuracy what would eventually happen to the

CIO. These observers included spokespersons for the AFL, the American Civil Liberties Union, the IWW, and the Communist Party of the United States, as well as A. J. Muste and many rank-and-file workers. William Forbath writes of the views of the AFL:

> As Furuseth, Frey, and the other AFL anti-injunction campaign veterans darkly prophesied, the Act inaugurated a regulatory regime that, in administering the new liberties, might resurrect many of the old restraints. If the old guard grossly underestimated the good that would flow from the new order, they were not wrong about the possibility that within it many of the old common-law restraints on collective action might reassert themselves. The federal courts have interpreted the NLRA [National Labor Relations Act] to prohibit virtually all forms of secondary strikes and boycotts, and the Supreme Court has upheld this bar against constitutional challenges.[37]

Still more incisive were the predictions of Roger Baldwin and Mary Van Kleeck, spokespersons for the American Civil Liberties Union (ACLU). In 1933, three days after the enactment of the National Industrial Recovery Act, Baldwin, the executive secretary of the ACLU, wrote to Secretary of Labor Frances Perkins expressing fear that the bituminous coal code might include the following objectionable features: (1) exclusive representational status for the majority union, (2) the dues check-off, and (3) the closed shop. Baldwin thought that all three provisions would have the effect of chilling the activities of minorities, such as the Progressive Miners, which was then contesting the hegemony of the United Mine Workers.[38]

In 1934, when the first version of the Wagner Act was proposed, Van Kleeck wrote Senator Robert Wagner advising him that the ACLU would oppose his bill because of the "inevitable trends of its administration." Fundamentally, Van Kleeck stated, "I believe that it is impossible 'to equalize the bargaining power of employers and employees,' since necessarily the decision to produce at all . . . rests with the employer." Under this condition of inequality, Van Kleeck went on:

> The danger is that the effort to regulate industrial relations by requiring of employers certain "fair practices," while appearing to impose those obligations upon them, necessarily brings the whole subject within the scope of governmental regulation. This involves a certain assumption as to a status quo. To prevent or discourage strikes which have for their purpose gradual increase in the workers' power in a period when fundamental economic

change in the ownership of industry can clearly be envisaged may only serve to check the rising power of the exponents of human rights, and indeed to protect private property rights in exchange for obligations which are likely to be merely the least common denominator of industrial practice.

Van Kleeck concluded by acknowledging that Senator Wagner's bill explicitly protected the right of workers to strike, but she insisted that "pressures would inevitably be exerted on the National Labor Relations Board to discourage strikes in favor of less disruptive methods of resolving conflicts."[39]

Van Kleeck's analysis of the proposed Wagner Act was echoed by Baldwin. In 1934 Baldwin wrote Senator David Walsh that the machinery proposed in the pending legislation would "impair labor's rights in the long run, however much its authors may intend precisely the contrary." In 1935 he wrote Senator Wagner that the ACLU would oppose creation of the National Labor Relations Board (NLRB) "on the ground that no such federal agency intervening in the conflicts between employers and employees can be expected to fairly determine the issues of labor's rights. We say this from a long experience with the various boards set up in Washington, all of which have tended to take from labor its basic right to strike by substituting mediation, conciliation, or, in some cases, arbitration." Baldwin urged Senator Wagner to consider "the view that the pressures on any government agency from employers are so constant and determined that it is far better to have no governmental intervention than to suffer the delusion that it will aid labor in its struggle for the rights to organize, bargain collectively and strike."[40]

Many rank-and-file workers expressed similar views. In the textile industry, employers used National Recovery Administration (NRA) boards to impose the hated stretch-out (where workers are required to do extra work for little or no additional pay), while workers boycotted the cotton textile labor board and shifted their struggle to the arena where they had more leverage—on the ground in the South. For textile workers, Janet Irons concludes, "government intervention proved disastrous."[41] Daniel Nelson maintains that rubber workers in Akron had concluded by early 1935 "that reliance on the government meant broken promises and endless delays."[42] C. J. Francis, the recording secretary of the National Match Workers' Council, wrote in like spirit to Francis Biddle, chair of the NLRB: "We cannot or at least will not use the agency set up by the Federal Government." Experience had taught these unionists that even a favorable decision would only lead to endless employer appeals. "We are not going to stand for this and as we see it, our only hope is through strike and to battle it out on the picket line," C. J. Francis declared.[43]

From the Beginning

Our view of the relationship between the alternative unionism of the early 1930s and the CIO is exemplified in an incident narrated by Peter Rachleff. In March 1937 at Albert Lea, Minnesota, truck drivers and warehouse workers went on strike. They were joined by Woolworth's clerks and workers at two plants of the American Gas Machine Company, who went on strike, and in the manner of that heroic spring, occupied their places of work. The Independent Union of All Workers coordinated all three actions. Every night the IUAW Drum and Bugle Corps paraded past each of the embattled work sites. The strikes held for two weeks. Then the sheriff and 150 special deputies stormed the offices of the IUAW and arrested sixty-two people. In response, 400 workers at nearby Hormel left their jobs and drove in a caravan to Albert Lea. As Rachleff recounts, "There they marched down the main street to the jail and demanded that all the prisoners be freed. When the brand new Albert Lea police cruiser pulled up, the crowd surrounded it, took the cops out, rolled it over, set it on fire, and then slid the charred remains into the lake across the street. Armed with crowbars, individuals from the crowd began to pry open the bars on the windows of the jail."[44]

Governor Elmer Benson, who had won election on the Farmer Labor ticket, thereupon appeared on the scene as a mediator. The settlement he proposed and eventually negotiated had three elements. First, all imprisoned workers were to be freed. Second, the company was to recognize and bargain with the IUAW. Third, *the IUAW was to affiliate with a national union within sixty days.* As it worked out, different IUAW local bodies joined different national unions, and the "one big union" at a city and regional level that the IUAW had nurtured for four years fell apart.

What did affiliation with a national union represent to the Albert Lea business community and to a governor anxious for social peace? Why was this chosen as the *quid* that would compensate the bosses for the *quo* of emptying the jails and agreeing to bargain?

Corporations like U.S. Steel at first responded to the labor ferment of the 1930s with a localized strategy. They formed local company unions or reasserted their traditional control of local communities through company-owned housing, company stores, and local governments staffed by company supervisors.[45] When coal miners turned up to picket with the steelworkers at U.S. Steel's Clairton coke works in 1933,[46] when independent federal local unions in Barberton marched on each other's picket lines in strike after strike from 1934 to 1936,[47] and when 170,000 southern textile workers, many of them organized in local "homegrown unions,"[48] showed that no part of the country was safe from the rank-and-file fever in 1934, then, in Janet Irons's words describing the Cotton Textile Institute, many corporations decided "to elevate the struggle to [a] national level. They hoped to thereby circumvent the local strategic leverage that mill workers had gained."[49]

Business came to recognize that the national union, whether AFL or CIO, with its vertical structure, its interest in a predictable cash flow from membership dues, and its demonstrated readiness to give away the right to strike and to police the shop floor, offered an alternative strategy of control perhaps more promising than the local company union. U.S. Steel espoused the new strategy in March 1937, in part, it seems, because "union firms had the advantage of avoiding the disruptions incident to conflict over unionization," as at Flint.[50] General Motors followed suit and became, in Ronald Edsforth's words, "a model for other large companies to follow in the 1940s."[51] [John Sargent emphasizes how "the companies became smart" and "realized that the best way to handle the situation was to work with the international leadership of this union."][52]

Accordingly, in contrast to those who emphasize the *difference* between the original CIO unions and what they became after World War II, we stress those features of national CIO unionism that *from the beginning* (or very shortly thereafter) distinguished CIO unionism at the national level from the horizontal, community-based unionism of the early 1930s.

First, national CIO unions were *from the beginning*, and aspired to be, "semipublic institutions, licensed by the state."[53] As government monopolies, they could insulate themselves from competing labor organizations by law instead of proving their superiority in practice or, as in European economies, sharing the representative function with other unions. This surrender of autonomy represented a fundamental departure from labor tradition in the United States.[54]

Second, national CIO unions *from the beginning* practiced top-down decision making. Independent local unions, such as the Independent Textile Union in Woonsocket, were typically led by people who continued to work at least part time in the shop. In contrast, the national CIO encouraged the proliferation of full-time officers and staff representatives, paid by the national union.[55]

Likewise the national CIO deliberately broke up militant local industrial unions like Local 65 of the Steelworkers in South Chicago and Local 156 of the UAW in Flint. Lizabeth Cohen narrates the disillusionment of George Patterson, who founded the Associated Employees at U.S. Steel South Works in Chicago and led it into the Steel Workers Organizing Committee (SWOC), where it became Local 65 of the United Steelworkers of America.

> Grassroots spontaneity and local concerns often were subordinated to the national CIO agenda. This imposition of "top-down" control happened first and most dramatically in steel, where the national leadership of SWOC began very early to tie the hands of its locals. At the start, district officers were appointed, not elected, and even after elections were held starting in 1944, it became virtually impossible to unseat District 31's director, Joe Germano. Locals also had little fiscal independence. Member dues went directly to the steel union's central office. As early as January 1937, Bittner was telling his organizers in Chicago, "We are dictating policy of all lodges until steel is organized. Democracy is important, but at this time collective bargaining and higher wages are the issues." When Bittner decided to divide South Works Local 65 into four, more controllable locals, . . . George Patterson . . . despaired: "Democracy from the bottom up, that we had practiced in Local 65, was now difficult to pursue. . . ." Steelworkers who had managed to overcome the fragmentation their employers had encouraged now had to contend with a union leadership also intent on dividing them. Similar frustration over lack of autonomy arose when the grievance committeemen elected by the different departments of South Works decided they would rather meet with the company's managers alone: "lo and behold, they found that there was always going to be a [SWOC] staff member coming into the meetings in order to see that the union would be guided." It did not take long for Patterson and other veterans of the Associated Employees to realize that "what we wanted" was not of concern to the men at the top. "They were hand-picking what we would call 'yes-men'; anybody that could stand and talk and didn't bow to their thinking was gradually eliminated."[56]

Ronald Edsforth tells a similar tale of the destruction of UAW Local 156 in Flint by the UAW and CIO hierarchies: "By the end of June [1937], Bob Travis and the rest of the local union's radical leadership had been removed from office and transferred to assignments that were deliberately scattered all over the country. Thousands of Flint workers protested this purge, but to no avail. A committee of five was put in charge of Local 156's affairs for the rest of the year. This committee, which contained no one from the union's radical 'Unity' caucus, cracked down on the militants within the auto plants."[57]

Third, whereas the rank-and-file unionism of the early 1930s emerged from and depended on direct action inside and outside the shop, national CIO unions *from the beginning* sought to regulate shop-floor activity from above and to prohibit shopfloor activity not approved at higher levels of the union. "In the next few years following the sit-downs, the main task" of the CIO was "to domesticate the popular insurgency," Steve Fraser writes. Thus, he explains, in Flint "a second conflict that pitted the International Union and GM management against rank-and-file shop-floor organizers supplanted the more celebrated battle between union and corporation. The emerging bureaucracy of the UAW took steps to dismantle the steward system, reduced the authority of local unions while augmenting the power of the International, and perfected the modern grievance procedure and committee system."[58]

Because they were separated from the shop floor and concerned about controlling it, national CIO leaders were insensitive to the shop floor's chief complaint: inhuman working conditions. Irons explains:

> Unions were now tied to an agenda set by the federal government rather than by their own membership. What the government determined to be legitimate grievances the union could fight for; what government policy ignored were inadmissible grievances. . . . [In 1938 the] new CIO-organized Textile Workers Organizing Committee (TWOC) encouraged southern workers to join unions because, thanks to the Wagner Act, the government was now behind them. But southern workers' protests against the stretch-out were ignored by the TWOC, as the union fought for goals that jibed more easily with government goals: increasing purchasing power and stable unions.[59]

Finally, *from the beginning* the national CIO leadership ardently sought to discourage independent labor politics and to tie the CIO to the Democratic Party. Eric Davin has brought to light the very substantial labor party movement during the early 1930s. In those years local labor parties fielded candidates in at least twenty-three communities and came to control the local government of at least one community, Berlin, New Hampshire. In at least ten other communities central labor unions endorsed the idea of a labor party, as did state federations of labor in Rhode Island, Vermont, New Jersey, and Wisconsin. At the 1935 AFL convention, where the Committee for Industrial Organization was created, a variety of unions submitted proposals for a labor party and a resolution to that effect failed by only a few votes.[60]

Early in 1936 John L. Lewis and Sidney Hillman founded Labor's Nonpartisan League, in the words of Steve Fraser, "as a way of circumventing third party movements."[61] A few weeks later, when the nascent UAW held a meeting in South Bend, defeated a resolution to back Roosevelt, and unanimously called for the formation of a farmer-labor party, Lewis directed Adolf Germer, the CIO staff representative, to strong-arm Homer Martin and the delegates into reconsidering.[62] During World War II, when third-party enthusiasm revived, the CIO created the Political Action Committee to "discourage every move in that direction."[63]

The Challenge of National Coordination

In presenting this view of the 1930s, we recognize that uncoordinated local disturbances could not have substituted for a national movement.[64] Alternative means were needed to coordinate local efforts on a regional and national scale.

Union activities in the 1930s suggest a variety of ways local unions can coordinate their efforts without belonging to the same organization and without sacrificing their freedom of action to the heavy-handed, top-down governance that has accompanied national unionism. The experience of Barberton, Ohio, during the half-century following the early 1930s indicates that such mechanisms can function effectively over a long period of time. Barberton workers created industry- or corporation-wide conferences, consisting of members of the same union working for the same company in different locations (the boilermakers), or members of different unions all employed by the same company (the chemical workers), or members of different unions in different companies of the same industry (the insulator workers).[65]

Similar schemes have been projected by paper workers and packinghouse workers in recent years. United Paperworkers Local 20 in Kaukana, Wisconsin, initiated a "coordinated bargaining pool" after losing a bitter eighteen-month strike against International Paper in 1987–88. Locals that joined the pool were to make common demands during their local negotiations, seal their ballots after the final contract vote, and work without a contract rather than take individual action or sign a concessionary agreement. When the pool felt it had sufficient strength, the ballots would be counted. If a majority voted against the local agreements, the union would take nationwide action. The strategy was intended to create a common expiration date and, ideally, one contract for all International Paper locations. By June 1991 the pool included 60 percent of International Paper workers in thirty-five locals. The strategy failed, not because of any substantive defect but because in December 1991 the NLRB declared it illegal.[66]

A Permanent Alternative

The evidence suggests that the horizontal style of unionism described in these essays remains a permanent alternative for the labor movement. Community-based or solidarity unionism is not a transitory phase or epiphenomenon, limited to a particular bygone stage of economic history. Consider Polish Solidarity. It originated in one of the more highly industrialized areas of Poland. It took the form of workplace committees with elected representatives from all departments, then of regional interfactory committees, but *not* a hierarchical national organization. Roman Laba argues persuasively that workers in the northern coastal cities of Gdansk, Gdynia, and Szczecin improvised the first two stages in this process in December 1970 to January 1971, without significant input from intellectuals. Workers built on this experience in the great upheaval of August 1980, challenging each other to recognize that, in the words of Anna Walentynowicz, "if the workers at these other factories were defeated, we wouldn't be safe either." At a meeting of rank-and-file delegates from all over Poland held on September 17, 1980, at the Seaman's Hotel in Wrzeszcz, there was a fierce debate between intellectuals associated with the workers' defense committee (KOR), who wanted a centralized national structure, and workers led by Lech Walesa, who wanted a decentralized structure grounded in many unions. The workers prevailed: Solidarity was to consist of "spreading horizontal structures."[67]

Nor is the alternative unionism described in these pages limited to the United States and Europe. Of many Latin American episodes of the same kind, the following is striking. In 1973 two hundred peasant families in Quebrada Seca, Honduras, occupied idle arable land. Soldiers were called to the site. As Gerald Schlabach recounts:

> The oldest men, the women, and children met the soldiers when they arrived. The military, as usual, first asked to speak with the group's leaders. [The people] replied that everyone was a leader, and whoever would speak would be speaking for all. The military men said they were there to negotiate, but that they wanted to

see the leaders so that they could go together to a meeting with INA [the National Agrarian Institute]. The people insisted that this was the place to negotiate, with everyone together.[68]

This book seeks to retrieve the memory of such experiences among workers in the United States. A curious set of union buttons or the stories told by grownups during one's own childhood offer clues to chunks of history forgotten by academia. As Eric Davin points out, historical amnesia can occur even among protagonists if they are never asked to recount their past struggles. He saw this "natural selection process" in action when a veteran of the woman suffrage movement was repeatedly asked by younger feminists to retell *that* past but was never called on to describe her role in the labor party movement of the 1930s: she remembered the first experience and forgot the second. Stan Weir offers other paradigms. He shows us Blackie and Chips, two veterans of the 1934 San Francisco general strike, systematically instructing younger seamen like Weir about the lessons of their experience. But Weir adds two things. First, he was able to grasp the most important lesson Blackie and Chips taught—that bureaucrats cannot reform themselves—only on the basis of his own experience in another general strike, in Oakland in 1946. Second, student activists in nearby Berkeley did in 1964 what Weir now wishes he had done himself in Oakland eighteen years earlier: they clambered onto a parked car and declared that since official leaders were not leading, a new leadership should be created from below.

Women, whether pecan shellers, textile workers, or garment workers, appear in these accounts as workers perhaps especially inclined to egalitarian, horizontally bonded forms of unionism. Other scholars who wish to explore and test the hypotheses set forth here might take note that several of these essays describe extraordinary experiences of black and white workers overcoming their differences in common struggle.

Top-down national union structures patterned on the corporation have failed. Local unions and their rank-and-file members, again prepared to be "all leaders," are needed to develop new forms of alternative unionism. We will not know if it is possible unless we try.

Afterword

Solidarity Unionism

As I labored on this manuscript, it was heartening to take note of a revival and more widespread exploration of the "solidarity unionism" that is front and center in Part II of these pages. Of course it is perilous to predict the future. Still, one would not have expected that major unions like the United Food and Commercial Workers (UFCW) or the Service Employees International Union (SEIU) would today be sponsoring campaigns among low-wage workers that ostensibly seek not to achieve exclusive bargaining status but to obtain immediate changes in particular conditions of employment through direct action.[1]

What appears to be going on is a belated response by the trade union movement to the relocation of manufacturing from the United States to other countries. So long as wages are dramatically lower on the Mexican side of the Rio Grande or in Bangladesh, that tectonic shift will continue. As a result, perhaps half of the jobs left in this country are in locations from which the work cannot be moved: among others, fast-food restaurants, warehousing, medical services, trucking, and public employment of all kinds.

The new economic geography requires new thinking on the part of the labor movement and its friends. It no longer suffices to make "union democracy" one's only objective. The election of reformers to positions of union leadership will not offer workers new leverage so long as collective bargaining agreements permit management to make unilateral investment decisions and the no-strike clause takes away from workers their only effective way to fight back.

Reflecting on the Walmart campaign of fall 2012, David Moberg observed in *In These Times*: "OUR Walmart's structure hearkens back to what historian Staughton Lynd called the 'alternative unionism' of the 1930s. These workers regarded everyone as a leader, acted locally without waiting for national union organizers and created local unions that were linked in horizontal solidarity rather than through subordination to a central hierarchy."[2]

The Walmart Campaign

Workers at the world's largest private employer, Walmart, have formed an organization called OUR (Organization United for Respect) Walmart. Their declaration said that they embraced a strong work ethic, compassion for one another, and honesty.

OUR Walmart criticized the company's so-called Open Door policy for receiving grievances on the grounds that (1) confidentiality is not respected; (2) a complaining worker is not allowed to bring a coworker as a witness; (3) the resolution of issues is not put in writing.

OUR Walmart also contested the employer's claim that it paid more than $13 an hour. The workers said that most of them made less than $10 an hour and that their schedules were often for only part-time work. In addition, although the company claimed that it provided health care, workers said that it took too many hours for a new worker to qualify and, even then, the employee's contribution was too expensive. OUR Walmart is backed by the United Food and Commercial Workers union.

At Walmart's warehouse hub in Elwood, Illinois, the supporting traditional union was the United Electrical Workers (UE). The facility processes a staggering 70 percent of Walmart's domestic goods. There were numerous safety issues. After workers tried to present a petition complaining about wage theft, poverty wages, the lack of set working schedules, and discrimination, just under thirty workers walked off the job. Supervisors tried to block their exit with forklifts. After three weeks and a massive outpouring of more than five hundred supporters at the remote site, strikers returned to work with discipline rescinded and with back pay for the days they were not at work.[3]

In 2012 on the day after Thanksgiving, there were protests at over one thousand Walmart stores in the United States. On December 14, 2012, there was a global day of action. Walmart employees in ten different countries took to the streets in marches, rallies, and protests. In Uruguay, India, South Africa, and the United Kingdom, workers delivered letters to their respective corporate offices demanding an end to repression.

In 2013 many Walmart employees took time off to attend the annual Walmart shareholders' meeting in Bentonville, Arkansas, and the corporation lashed back with discipline and discharges. Also, in November 2013 Walmart management in Canton, Ohio, elicited incredulity and contempt when it asked its employees to donate food so that "Associates [Walmartese for 'employees'] in Need can enjoy Thanksgiving Dinner."

$15 an Hour

Even more ambitiously, the Service Employees union has sought to reach out to fast-food workers with a demand for $15 an hour.

None of the more than 200,000 fast-food restaurants in the United States are unionized. And contrary to a familiar stereotype, it is no longer the case that fast-food workers are overwhelmingly single teenagers. An August 2013 study by the Center for Economic Policy and Research in Washington, DC, found that 40 percent of fast-food workers are 25 or older, and more than a quarter of fast-food workers are raising children. The average fast-food worker is a woman twenty-eight years old.

As is true of the new unionism generally, fast-food workers are for the time being not seeking a comprehensive contract or exclusive collective bargaining status but increased pay. Robert Schwartz, an experienced commentator on shopfloor strategies, has asked in *Labor Notes* whether "working without a contract" is "a strategy whose time has come." Schwartz explained that when a contract expires, union members who simply go on working gain the right to strike and "greatly enhanced rights to bargain over day-to-day management decisions." In other words, in the absence of contract clauses requiring deference to management's authority and prohibiting strikes and slowdowns, the employer's ability to make decisions unilaterally becomes much more difficult to enforce.[4]

Beginning in Manhattan in November 2012, one-day strikes during peak mealtimes seeking $15 an hour spread to Chicago and Washington and then to St. Louis, Kansas City, Detroit, Flint, and the West Coast. Companies like McDonald's, Taco Bell, Popeye's, and Long John Silver's have been picketed.

According to Mary Kay Henry, SEIU president, the campaign reflects the belief of union members that economic inequality is the nation's number-one problem. The effort, she asserted, is about "How do we shift things in the entire low-wage economy?" She has also said: "Our primary goal is to help workers boost wages. We think a key part of that is helping workers form organizations where they can directly bargain for wages with their employers." The question of whether fast-food strikers would eventually join the Service Employees union, according to Ms. Henry, has been "kicked down the road."

Is the New Unionism Top-Down or Bottom-Up?

In fall 2013, after about a year of highly publicized activity by low-wage workers, the question began to be raised whether these campaigns were really as spontaneous and bottom-up as they were made to appear.

Writing in *In These Times*, Arun Gupta, former coeditor of the national Occupy newspaper, began by conceding that the SEIU-backed campaign had "set in motion thousands of working poor, mainly African Americans and Latinos, who are acting collectively to better their lives."[5] Asking, "Why fast-food and why now?," Gupta asserted that "it's where a dying labor movement sees most opportunity." Private-sector union density is now 6.6 percent, he continued. The fast-food industry in the United States employs more than four million workers who earned an average of $8.72 an hour in 2010.

According to union spokespersons, these objective circumstances explain the uprising of fast-food workers that unions like the SEIU "support." However, Gupta talked to more than twenty organizers and workers involved in the campaign for $15 an hour who, speaking in confidence, told a different story. The official version was that organizers seeking to halt planned school closings or to resist bus-fare hikes kept hearing from residents of low-income neighborhoods that fast-food jobs were "keeping them poor." But three former organizers in Chicago and two former organizers in New York told Gupta that SEIU was not only funding the organizing but directing the campaign. While "SEIU maintains that Fight for 15 is a bottom-up project, the organizers who did the legwork concluded that SEIU funded and directed it from early on."

Organizers for SEIU were given daily quotas of signatures on petitions. Carlos (not his real name) said that SEIU recognized that its name "has a lot of baggage" and so wanted to funnel the effort "through smaller organizations so it looks like more of a grassroots effort." A decision to stage a low-wage walkout in Chicago on April 24, 2013, was made at a meeting to which New York workers were flown by SEIU. Other organizers told Gupta that for the SEIU it was "just a question of going through the motions of getting people to come to the decisions that they want them to." Similarly, the decision to conduct a 60-city walkout on August 29, 2013, was made at a convention in Detroit on August 15–16 at which SEIU brought together "about 700 low-wage workers, organizers and staff from around the country." Public relations firms have been hired to generate publicity. According to Gupta, there is little evidence of worker-to-worker organizing except in Chicago.

What should we make of this? Readers who, like myself, are familiar with the work of organizations created by Saul Alinsky and those trained by him, will recognize some familiar practices. Gupta rightly puts special emphasis on the fact that the long-term goals of all this low-wage-worker activity are vague. So it was also at the Industrial Areas Foundation Training Institute where I was employed for a time in the early 1970s. Bringing a protest organization into existence always had higher priority than what the organization would do with whatever leverage it was able to acquire.

On the other hand, think of the lack of "national coordination" emphasized in several of the essays in the long section of this book on labor organizing from below. That is the element that John L. Lewis, and money and organizers from the United Mine Workers, provided to fledgling CIO unions in the late 1930s. It is what the UFCW, the SEIU, and the UE have provided to local low-wage insurgencies in recent years.

What we confront is not a new problem. It is the old problem of how to transform the capitalist system without sacrificing ideals of participatory decision making.

This problem presented itself in the encounter of local soviets and factory committees with the Bolshevik Party in 1917 and thereafter; in Spain in the 1930s; in France in 1968; in Polish Solidarity; and in the United Farm Workers union in its relationship to Cesar Chavez.

I do not have a generalized answer. What I will try to do in the next few pages is to offer certain specific suggestions that might open doors in practice to at least partial solutions.

The Labor Board, the Dues Check-off, Minority Unionism, Class Solidarity, and Community Support

There has been much discussion of the failure of the National Labor Relations Act, enacted in 1935, to provide substantial protection to working people and their organizations in the face of the management offensive beginning in the 1970s. Some trade union officials went so far as to condemn the NLRB as useless and to call for the repeal of the NLRA (or, as it was called after amendment in 1947, the Labor Management Relations Act).

My own position and that of my colleague Daniel Gross is different. We agree that Section 9 of the NLRA, setting forth the process whereby a union can become the exclusive representative of workers in an appropriate bargaining unit, provides a road better *not* taken. (See the alternative of "minority unionism," discussed below.) However, we think that

Sections 7 and 8 of the Act, affirming the right to "concerted activity for mutual aid or protection" and describing how aggrieved workers can file an unfair labor practice (ULP) charge when they believe their Section 7 rights have been violated, remain invaluable.[6]

Of course, as Gupta argues, when workers stop work to protest the unfair discharge of a fellow worker and simply refuse to perform until their colleague has been reinstated, such direct action is to be preferred. Yet that option is not always available, and to step aside without response when a discharge occurs is unacceptable. So Gross and I believe that although it takes too long and, even when successful, provides inadequate compensation together with reinstatement, the possibility of filing a ULP charge remains a hard-won achievement that should not be discarded.

The usefulness of this strategy was apparent in a preliminary decision of the National Labor Relations Board in November 2013.[7] Initially Walmart had hesitated to punish employees who walked off the job or protested in other ways. However, the NLRB found that during 2013 Walmart had illegally disciplined and fired several dozen employees for their protest activity in more than a dozen states, including California, Colorado, Texas, and Massachusetts.

The issues of dues check-off and "minority" or "members-only" unionism are interlocked. There are experienced trade unionists who consider that without the dues check-off, many workers would be "free riders"—that is, could enjoy the benefits of a collective bargaining agreement for their workplace without paying for them. On the other hand, there are union veterans like Sylvia Woods who recalled that in her Bendix plant during World War II: "We never had check-off. We didn't want it. We said if you have a closed shop and check-off, everybody sits on their butts and they don't have to worry about organizing and they don't care what happens."[8]

The answer to this dilemma may be minority unionism. Vicki Starr (aka Stella Nowicki) remembered that workers in the "beef kill" of meatpacking plants in Chicago in the 1930s "were the best organized and most militant. . . . And if this department went down, the whole plant went down."[9] If such highly skilled workers in a critical part of the production process can achieve a change in their working conditions through direct action and subsequent negotiation with the employer, their example may induce other workers to become union members and to pay dues voluntarily.

The foremost advocate for minority unionism is labor law professor Charles J. Morris. In a book published in 2005, Morris maintained that under the National Labor Relations Act an employer has a legal duty to "bargain with a labor union representing less than a majority of the firm's employees." He credits another labor law professor, Clyde Summers, with recognizing that while Section 9 of the NLRA makes a majority union the "exclusive representative" of all the employees in a bargaining unit, Section 7 of the Act more fundamentally entitles workers to "bargain collectively through representatives of their own choosing," drawing no distinctions between majority unions and minority unions. In a later article, Professor Morris argued that the need for minority or members-only unions "has been dramatically evidenced by recent work stoppages at various Wal-Mart and fast-food locations."[10]

In some cities low-wage workers have been forming workers' centers like the Workers' Solidarity Club of Youngstown that bring together workers from many different places of work and address class-wide concerns. My experience is that in such a group there is little need to propagandize for a class approach to issues, because that approach is implicit in the varied identities of the persons in the room. Groups of this kind nurture solidarity horizontally as workers join one another's picket lines and undertake collective actions. Moreover, such groups, bringing together workers who do different kinds of work, can undertake legislative lobbying for objectives like raising the minimum wage.[11]

It must finally be emphasized that community support is an essential component of the new unionism. The workers for fast-food companies and other low-wage employers are notoriously transient. Persistent support by a surrounding community that is *not* mobile may be the component that makes success possible.

It has long been recognized that workers are most likely to act in solidarity when they are not only colleagues on the job but also neighbors off the clock. Seamen are an obvious example: they work and also live in enforced proximity twenty-four hours a day. Miners, such as coal miners, live and work in isolated settings that produce a similar three-dimensional solidarity. Lumber workers, the "timber beasts" of IWW legend, as well as soldiers in combat and prisoners, likewise exist in settings of continuous enforced contact that strengthen the capacity to resist.

Whether or not the workplace itself is set apart as in the foregoing instances, there are enormous opportunities for community actions in support of workplace self-activity. Most low-wage and service employments offer the public a final product. That product can be boycotted by members of a community acting under the protection of the First Amendment. A well-remembered instance in Youngstown concerned a Buick service and sales enterprise. The state court judge forbade more than two strikers at any entrance: even a fellow worker bringing coffee to two picketers might find himself or herself cited for contempt. Protesters thereupon improvised a tactic later referred to as the "honkathon." At times of particularly heavy sales activity, like Saturday afternoon, supporters drove their cars slowly down the main street adjoining the Buick establishment honking their horns. Signs hung from the car windows described the employer in colorful terms. Driven frantic by the honkathons, the employer settled.

The activities and practices discussed above display a kinship with the approach of the Industrial Workers of the World (IWW) in the years preceding World War I. A variety of young people are seeking to revive the IWW itself.

History from Below as Accompaniment

In a small book titled *Accompanying* (PM Press, 2012), I proposed "accompaniment" as the desirable form of relationship between the person with a professional skill (such as doctor, teacher, lawyer, clergyperson) and the poor and working people they seek to assist. Similarly, I think those who do history from the bottom up also should seek to accompany.

What would this mean? Archbishop Oscar Romero, who seems to have initiated this use of the term *accompaniment*, emphasized listening. Indeed history practiced as a form of accompaniment would become a process of learning together. New ideas, rather than being closely guarded as means to personal professional advancement, would be set out in the open as hypotheses. These hypotheses would be tested by oneself and others through (in the case of recent history) new interviews and (in all cases) discovery and review of hitherto unused documents.

Understood in this way, the practice of history from below would become a way of nurturing community among persons sharing the same or similar experiences. The exchange of ideas about the past could serve as rituals of renewed affirmation concerning the future. But in contrast to patriotic rituals the meaning of which has been fixed in advance, this sort of sharing would be flexible and would encompass new reflections at each repetition.

In Youngstown, Ohio, near which I live, there is a museum known as "the steel museum" that houses items recalling the days when the city was one of the leading steel-producing communities in the United States.

When my wife and I moved to the Youngstown area in 1976, steel mills operated in continuous shifts, and grocery stores were open twenty-four hours a day. At the very center of downtown Youngstown, where streets intersected to enclose an oval of open ground, there stood an historical marker of the Little Steel Strike of 1937. The words on the marker memorialized an encounter between striking workers and the authorities on June 20, 1937, which left fourteen workers injured and two dead. One year, Ed Mann obtained from IWW national headquarters a packet of Joe Hill's ashes, and members of the Workers' Solidarity Club scattered them at the foot of the marker.

Traffic patterns at the Youngstown city center were frequently re-engineered in an effort to restore, in this mechanical way, the more lively downtown of yesteryear. In one such makeover the Little Steel Strike plaque disappeared. After a good deal of inquiry, its location was discovered. Now it stands about sixty feet from the steel museum parking lot, at an angle that requires a special effort to see it from close up. In fall 2012 the marker was covered with pigeon droppings.

History from below would seek to reverse the process. It would reject the apprehensions of the Chamber of Commerce that attention to past labor strife would inhibit present economic growth. It would recognize the Little Steel Strike as the spiritual heart of the community's history.

I have done history at the New York Public Library and, at the New York Historical Society, sitting in a room with a microfilm reader and scouring every newspaper published in New York City between 1783 and 1788. I have also done history, tape recorder in hand, venturing throughout the Mahoning Valley of Ohio in search of firsthand experiences relevant to the closing of U.S. Steel mills in the area, or trying to tease out the exact sequence of events in a prison uprising.

All these procedures are legitimate ways to do history. But the process outside the library is more three-dimensional and of necessity involves persons in addition to oneself in trying to understand what really happened.

I believe history from the bottom up has barely begun.

Notes

Preface and Acknowledgments

1. History News Network has published a bibliography of the controversy
   through mid-November 2013 titled "HNN Hot Topics: The Howard Zinn
   Debate." Listed are nine items "For the Prosecution" and four "For the
   Defense." An example of such exchanges is David Greenberg, "Agit-Prof:
   Howard Zinn's Influential Mutilations of American History," and in response,
   Jesse Lemisch, Robert Cohen, and Staughton Lynd, "Rebutting David Green-
   berg's Broadside on Howard Zinn," *History News Network*, March 19, 2013.
   Another item I wrote that appears in the bibliography is "The Howard Zinn
   I Remember," an "edited version of a letter sent to his friends and colleagues,"
   http://hnn.us/article/123066. See also Sam Wineburg, "Undue Certainty:
   Where Howard Zinn's *People's History* Falls Short," *American Educator*,
   Winter 2012–13, and my response, http://zinnedproject.org/2013/03/re-
   sponsebystaughtonlynd/.
2. Thomas J. Humphrey, "Leases and the Laboring Classes in Revolutionary
   America," in *Class Matters: Early North America and the Atlantic World*, ed.
   Simon Middleton and Billy G. Smith (Philadelphia: University of Pennsylvania Press, 2008), 183.
3. I should like to acknowledge Roslyn Sims of Youngstown as the person who
   suggested, in a talk my wife and I attended in 1991, that the experience of
   Native Americans and African Americans amounted to a "holocaust." Roz
   lost one whole side of her family in the Holocaust of World War II. Her husband was an African American steelworker. She insisted, "There was more
   than one holocaust." And Noel Ignatiev prodded me to try to view the world
   through the eyes of the most exploited and vulnerable.
4. Alfred F. Young, Gary Nash, and Ray Raphael, eds., *Revolutionary Founders:
   Rebels, Radicals, and Reformers in the Making of the Nation* (New York:
   Alfred A. Knopf, 2011), 4–5.
5. James Kirby Martin, "Forgotten Heroes of the Revolution," in ibid., 211.
6. Staughton Lynd, "The Compromise of 1787," in *Class Conflict, Slavery, and*

the United States Constitution, rev. ed. (Cambridge: Cambridge University Press, 2009), 185–213.

7. Nick Turse, *Kill Anything That Moves: The Real American War in Vietnam* (New York: Henry Holt, 2013), 3–4, 17; Trent Angers, *The Forgotten Hero of My Lai: The Hugh Thompson Story* (Lafayette, LA: Acadian House, 1999), chap. 6.

8. Leon Trotsky, *The History of the Russian Revolution*, trans. Max Eastman (Ann Arbor: University of Michigan Press, 1932), 1:102.

9. Frank Bardacke, *Trampling Out the Vintage: Cesar Chavez and the Two Souls of the United Farm Workers* (London: Verso, 2011), 1–13.

10. Viktor E. Frankl, *Man's Search for Meaning* (Boston: Beacon, 2006), 6.

11. Statement Suspending the Third Hunger Strike, posted on September 5, 2013. In the author's possession.

12. Letter to Staughton Lynd, September 29, 2013. During the Attica rebellion in 1971, observer Tom Wicker asked himself: "Could he be seeing in D-yard . . . that class interest might overcome racial animosities? Was it possible that the dregs of the earth, in a citadel of the damned, somehow in the desperation of human need had cast aside all the ancient and encumbering trappings of racism to find in degradation the humanity they knew at last they shared?" Tom Wicker, *A Time to Die* (New York: Quadrangle, 1975), 238.

Part I: Introduction

1. E. P. Thompson, *The Making of the English Working Class* (London: Victor Gollancz, 1963), 9, 12.

2. Eric Foner, Jesse Lemisch, and Manning Marable, "The Historical Scholarship of Herbert Aptheker," in *African American History and Radical Scholarship*, ed. Herbert Shapiro (Marxist Educational Press, 1998), 74–75.

3. See my essay "The Webbs, Lenin, Rosa Luxemburg," in Staughton Lynd, *Living inside Our Hope* (Ithaca, NY: Cornell University Press, 1997), 263n24.

4. Jay Winter, *Dreams of Peace and Freedom: Utopian Moments in the Twentieth Century* (New Haven, CT: Yale University Press, 2006), 153–54.

5. See, generally, Martin Duberman, *Howard Zinn: A Life on the Left* (New York: New Press, 2012), chaps. 3–5, 7, 9–11.

Edward Thompson's Warrens

1. The following is a portion of the E. P. Thompson Memorial Lecture delivered at the University of Pittsburgh in November 2000.

2. I should like to thank Peter Linebaugh for locating this hard-to-find essay and sending me a copy.

3. "Socialist Humanism: An Epistle to the Philistines," *The New Reasoner* (1957), 105, 106, 107, 110, 139 (references to "transition"), 140 (Trotskyism).

4. "Homage to Tom Maguire," in *Making History: Writings on History and Culture* (New York: W. W. Norton, 1994), 24, 26; Sheila Rowbotham quoted in Bryan D. Palmer, *Objections and Oppositions: The Histories and Politics of E. P. Thompson* (London: Verso, 1994), 91.

5. The essays are "At the Point of Decay" and "Revolution," in *Out of Apathy* (London: Stevens, 1960), 3–15, 287–308.
6. "At the Point of Decay," 6; "Outside the Whale," also in *Out of Apathy*, 194.
7. "Revolution," 294, 296.
8. Ibid., 300–301. The late Marty Glaberman called my attention to a similar passage in Trotsky's *History of the Russian Revolution*, ed. Max Eastman (Ann Arbor: University of Michigan Press, 1932), 3:168–69, wherein Trotsky argued that the proletariat lacks the "social advantages" that a network of prerevolutionary institutions gave the bourgeoisie and "can count only on its numbers, its solidarity, its cadres, its official staff."
9. Ibid., 301–02.
10. Ibid., 303.
11. Ibid., 304–05.
12. "The Peculiarities of the English," in *The Poverty of Theory and Other Essays* (New York: Monthly Review, 1978), 281–82.
13. Ibid., 282.

Howard Zinn

1. Howard Zinn, *You Can't Be Neutral on a Moving Train: A Personal History of Our Times* (Boston: Beacon, 1994), 181.
2. Ibid., 90.
3. Ibid., 94–95.
4. Ibid., 92–94.
5. Ibid., 95.
6. *Howard Zinn on War*, ed. Marilyn B. Young (New York: Seven Stories, 2011), 14–17.
7. Howard Zinn, *A Power Governments Cannot Suppress* (San Francisco: City Lights Books, 2007), 91.
8. Howard Zinn, *Just War* (Milan: Edizione Charta, 2005), 14.
9. Howard Zinn, *Howard Zinn Speaks: Collected Speeches 1962–2009*, ed. Anthony Arnove (Chicago: Haymarket Books, 2012), 284–95.
10. Zinn, *You Can't Be Neutral*, 180.
11. Ibid., 91–92.
12. George Sullivan, "Working for Survival," in *Rank and File: Personal Histories by Working-Class Organizers*, ed. Alice Lynd and Staughton Lynd, expanded ed. (Chicago: Haymarket Books, 2011), 209.
13. The following discussion of the influence of Popular Front ideology on Howard Zinn is based partly on personal experience. The best scholarly discussion I have encountered is in Michael Kazin, *American Dreamers: How the Left Changed a Nation* (New York: Vintage Books, 2011), e.g., xi–xiii (Dr. Seuss), 157–60 (Popular Front culture), 176–84 ("This Land Is *Our* Land").
14. Zinn, *You Can't Be Neutral*, 170–71.
15. See Laurie Levinger, *Love and Revolutionary Greetings: An Ohio Boy in the Spanish Civil War* (Eugene, OR: Resource Publications, 2012).
16. Edmund S. Morgan, *Inventing the People: The Rise of Popular Sovereignty in England and America* (New York: W. W. Norton, 1988), 13, 153.

17. Howard Zinn, introduction to *Harvey Wasserman's History of the United States* (orig. New York: Harper and Row, 1972; repr. Columbus, OH: www. harveywasserman.com books, 2004), v.
18. Ibid., vii, emphasis mine.
19. *You Can't Be Neutral*, 173.
20. Howard Zinn, *The Politics of History* (Urbana: University of Illinois Press, 1970), 100.
21. In a book titled *Accompanying: Pathways to Social Change* (Oakland, CA: PM Press, 2012), I wrote that the earliest example I could find of a contrast between the 1 and 99 percents was an article published in February 2010. But I now think I was wrong, because in the twentieth-anniversary edition of *A People's History*, published in 1999, on p. 646 Howard is already contrasting these two groups.
22. *People's History*, 659.
23. *You Can't Be Neutral*, 176–77.
24. Ibid., 179–80.
25. *People's History*, 399–402.
26. Ibid., 402.
27. *You Can't Be Neutral*, 190–92.

Part II: Introduction

1. Robin L. Einhorn, "Forty Years Later: A New Foreword," in Staughton Lynd, *Class Conflict, Slavery, and the United States Constitution*, new ed. (Cambridge: Cambridge University Press, 2009), xi. This volume contained my essay on the Northwest Ordinance. Cambridge University Press simultaneously issued a new edition of my *Intellectual Origins of American Radicalism*, first published by Pantheon in 1968.
2. See again Staughton Lynd, "The Compromise of 1787," in *Class Conflict, Slavery, and the United States Constitution*, 185–213. At roughly the same time that I gave up on getting a job as a history teacher, I wrote very rough drafts of two essays on the American Revolution.After starting law school I forgot about them. But they were saved by my mentor and friend Alfred Young and, after I did very substantial reworking along with my new friend David Waldstreicher, published as Lynd and Waldstreicher, "Free Trade, Sovereignty, and Slavery: Toward an Economic Interpretation of American Independence," *William and Mary Quarterly*, 3rd ser., 68, no. 4 (October 2011): 597–656.
3. Staughton Lynd, *The Fight against Shutdowns: Youngstown's Steel Mill Closings* (San Pedro, CA: Singlejack Books, 1982).
4. Staughton Lynd, *Lucasville: The Untold Story of a Prison Uprising*, 2nd ed. (Oakland: PM Press, 2011).
5. See Staughton Lynd, *Accompanying: Pathways to Social Change* (Oakland: PM Press, 2013), 53.

Guerilla History in Gary

1. In his account of union organization in steel, *As Steel Goes*, Robert R. R. Brooks states, "It was perfectly clear that the issue was not written agreements or signed contracts, but unionism versus antiunionism." But Brooks goes on to provide evidence undercutting his own statement and corroborating Smith and Brown. The Little Steel corporations in the Chicago area were Inland, Youngstown Sheet and Tube, and Republic. Brooks writes of the Youngstown Sheet and Tube plants in the Mahoning Valley: "[By January 1940] S.W.O.C. claimed a majority of employees as members, had set up grievance adjustment machinery which was informally recognized by the company and frequently conferred with plant officials in the settlement of individual grievances. In some respects the union was better off than in many U.S. Steel plants since it was not bound by a contract to confine its grievance claims to matters covered by the contract. It was able, therefore, to press and sometimes win grievance claims which under the standard contract would be thrown out in the early stages of adjustment." And Brooks states of union-management relations in Republic Steel at the same time: "Since there are not contractual provisions to the contrary, national officers of the S.W.O.C. may and do take individual grievances over the heads of foremen to the plant managers." Brooks's authority for both of these statements is Jack Mayo, a SWOC subregional director. As for Inland, a master's essay by Jack Stein of the University of Chicago on "A History of Unionization in the Steel Industry in the Chicago Area," states of the precontract period: "At the Inland plant in Indiana Harbor . . . the workers claimed that they had a better setup than in many of the plants of the United States Steel Corporation."

The Possibility of Radicalism in the Early 1930s: The Case of Steel

1. C. Wright Mills, *The New Men of Power: America's Labor Leaders* (New York, 1948), 224. A few of the notes to this article as it originally appeared in *Radical America* and in the volume *Workers' Struggles, Past and Present* have been condensed. I should like to acknowledge the generosity of Professor Carroll Moody in sharing his own research.
2. Mark Naison, "The Southern Tenant Farmers' Union and the CIO," *Radical America* 2, no. 5 (September-October 1968): 53.
3. Art Preis, *Labor's Giant Step: Twenty Years of the CIO* (New York, 1972), chap. 4.
4. Jeremy Brecher, *Strike!* (San Francisco, 1975), chap. 5 and throughout.
5. Staughton Lynd, "Prospects for the New Left," *Liberation,* Winter 1971, 20.
6. Compare Carroll Daugherty, Melvin de Chazeau, and Samuel Stratton, *The Economics of the Iron and Steel Industry* (New York and London, 1937), 2:947n; Vincent D. Sweeney, *The United Steelworkers of America Twenty Years Later* (n.p., n.d.), 7; and Harvey O'Connor, Federated Press dispatch, April 30, 1934, Columbia University.
7. Harvey O'Connor, "Personal Histories of the Early CIO," *Radical America* 5

(May–June 1971): 52–55.

8. My authority for this statement is a novel written by a steelworker which very closely follows the events of the 1930s and includes extracts from the minutes of the company union at the Edgar Thomson Works. Thomas Bell, *Out of This Furnace* (New York, 1950), 290.

9. Walter Galenson, *The CIO Challenge to the AFL: A History of the American Labor Movement, 1935–1941* (Cambridge, 1960), 75.

10. Ibid., 94.

11. David J. McDonald, *Union Man* (New York, 1969), 93ff.

12. This account of the captive mine strike of 1933 is based on almost-daily dispatches of reporters for the Federated Press, July–December 1933; Harvey O'Connor, *Steel—Dictator* (New York, 1935), chap. 14; Irving Bernstein, *Turbulent Years: A History of the American Worker, 1933–1941* (Boston, 1971), 49–61; and Muriel Sheppard, *Cloud by Day: The Story of Coal and Coke and People* (Chapel Hill, 1947), chap. 10.

13. Harold Ruttenberg, "Steel Labor, the NIRA, and the Amalgamated Association," a detailed narrative of the rank-and-file movement of 1934 (Ruttenberg Papers, Pennsylvania State University). Unless otherwise indicated, statements about the 1934 movement are based on this source.

14. Robert R. R. Brooks, *As Steel Goes . . . : Unionism in a Basic Industry* (New Haven, 1940), chap. 3. This is an extraordinary interview, but must be used with care. Brooks interviewed Clarence Irwin, for Mrs. Irwin remembers the occasion. But the text of the so-called interview as published in *As Steel Goes . . .* draws on several sources, as Brooks explicitly acknowledges. See his footnote on p. 262.

15. Interview with Heber Blankenhorn, Columbia University Oral History Project, 437a and 438a.

16. Daugherty, de Chazeau, and Stratton, *Economics of Iron and Steel Industry*, 2:659n.

17. As of the date this article was written, the rank and file of the United Steelworkers of America had repeatedly attempted to modify the USWA constitution in these same three ways—referendum vote on new contracts, election of staff, local right to strike—and repeatedly failed.

18. O'Connor, "Personal Histories of the Early CIO."

19. This account of the SMWIU is based on Horace B. Davis, *Labor and Steel* (New York, 1933), especially 257–58 and 264, and on interviews with three SMWIU organizers.

20. Address by Leon Callow, former SMWIU organizer in Youngstown, at Youngstown State University, April 14, 1972.

21. SMWIU, leaflet headlined "Steel Workers! Organize and Prepare to Strike!" in O'Connor Papers, no date (May or early June 1934).

22. Clarence Irwin to Harold Ruttenberg, May 17, 1934, exhibit 10 attached to Ruttenberg's narrative.

23. Blankenhorn interview, Columbia University Oral History Project, 444a. In Daugherty, de Chazeau, and Stratton, *Economics of the Iron and Steel Industry*, 2:1059, the statement is made that one or more of the Big Four persuaded the rank-and-file leaders to "turn down united-front offer from

Leftwing Steel and Metal Workers" on May 20. Ruttenberg was a student of Daugherty's and did research for this study.

24. The quoted words are identical to words that Ruttenberg, in his narrative, has himself saying to Forbeck: "Number 3 (Ruttenberg) told Forbeck that they wanted to institutionalize the whole affair," and so forth.

25. Cecil Allen, open letter to "Fellow Steel Workers" (undated, but around July 1, 1934), exhibit 34 attached to Ruttenberg's narrative. The Weirton leaders had been to Washington prior to May 1934 to testify on their own behalf before the National Labor Board. As early as April, Bill Spang stated: "We're tired of sending delegations to Washington and of the endless run-around we get there." Federated Press dispatch, April 18, 1934.

26. Statement by James Egan to Harold Ruttenberg on June 5, 1934, Ruttenberg narrative, p. 23. That same day, an SMWIU delegation in Washington voiced the same criticism to the press. Federated Press dispatch, June 5, 1934.

27. Harold Ruttenberg to George Soule, July 6, 1934, Ruttenberg Papers.

28. Arthur S. Weinberg interview with Ruttenberg, May 12, 1968, and Don Kennedy interview with Ruttenberg, April 24, 1969, Pennsylvania State Oral History Project.

29. In an interview on March 30, 1972, John Morris stated that he had been hired by the Calumet Protective Association at its office on the fifth floor of the Hotel Gary, issued a uniform and a gun, and housed in the Youngstown Sheet and Tube mill in East Chicago, Indiana, for three days before the Amalgamated special convention in mid-June 1934.

30. Harold Ruttenberg, "The Special Convention."

31. Bell, *Out of This Furnace*, 323–24.

32. Clarence Irwin to "Dear Brother," November 19, 1934, NSLRB files. This was an invitation to a secret meeting of representatives from several districts of the Amalgamated with SMWIU representatives in Cleveland on November 25.

33. Clarence Irwin to Harold Ruttenberg, January 23, 1935, Ruttenberg Papers, and Harvey O'Connor to Clarence Irwin, February 12, 1935, O'Connor Papers.

34. *Youngstown Vindicator*, February 8, 1935, Irwin scrapbook.

35. *Pittsburgh Post Gazette*. February 4, 1935, Ruttenberg Papers.

36. At the convention, a careful check determined that the rank-and-file delegates present represented about 50,000 expelled members. Federated Press dispatches, March 28 and April 2, 29, and 30, 1935.

37. Federated Press dispatch, February 5, 1935.

38. *Daily Worker*, April 15, 1935.

39. Federated Press dispatch, March 28, 1935.

40. Federated Press dispatches, April 1 and 2, 1935.

41. Harold Ruttenberg, "A Rank-and-File Strike," Ruttenberg Papers; Federated Press dispatches, May 29 and 31 and June 3, 4, and 5, 1935. Clarence Irwin was fired as a result of this strike and thereafter worked full time first for the rank-and-file movement and then for SWOC. Brooks, *As Steel Goes . . .*, 70.

42. Federated Press dispatches, June 3 and 14, July 1, 5, and 29, and August 22, 1935.

43. Federated Press dispatch, April 2, 1935.
44. Blankenhorn interview, Columbia University Oral History Project, 475a; Federated Press dispatches, April 19 and May 4, 1935.
45. A group of rank-and-file steelworkers confronted Lewis when he spoke at Greensburg, Pennsylvania, April 1, 1936, and demanded that he make good on his rhetoric about organizing steel. Lewis invited a committee of three to meet with himself and the CIO executive committee in Washington the next week. The result was the decision to offer $500,000 to the Amalgamated convention meeting in Canonsburg, Pennsylvania, on April 28. There are accounts of the April 1 encounter in Brooks, *As Steel Goes . . .* ,71–72; by Albert Atallah in an interview with Alice Hoffman, September 20, 1967, Pennsylvania State Oral History Project; and by George Powers, in *Monongahela Valley: Cradle of Steel Unionism* (East Chicago, Ind., 1972). My statement about the connection of the Communist Party with this event is based on an interview with a participant.
46. "Foster, who should know, wrote later that 60 of the first organizers hired by SWOC were members of the Communist Party." Len DeCaux, *Labor Radical: From the Wobblies to CIO* (Boston, 1971), 279.
47. Brooks, *As Steel Goes . . .* ,157 and 177, and DeCaux, *Labor Radical,*280.
48. Statements made to Harvey O'Connor at the February 3, 1935, meeting, Federated Press dispatch, February 3, 1935.
49. *Daily Worker*, March 2 and July 24, 1935.
50. Press clippings in Irwin scrapbook, March 31, 1936, and May 21, 1939.

"We Are All Leaders"
The Alternative Unionism of the Early 1930s

1. Victor Reuther, prefatory note to Robert S. Lynd, *You Can Do It Better Democratically* (Detroit: UAW-CIO Education Department, 1949).
2. Lloyd Ulman, *The Rise of the National Trade Union: The Development and Significance of Its Structure, Governing Institutions and Economic Policies* (Cambridge: Harvard University Press, 1955), 27–32, 37–42. The thesis that union structure follows market development is generally shared by authors of the Commons-Perlman school of labor history. See, for instance, Selig Perlman, *A History of Trade Unionism in the United States* (1922; reprint, New York: Augustus Kelley, 1950), 109–10.
3. Melvyn Dubofsky writes: "In examining the 1930s, how should we go about creating the history of that era? Two convenient models are at hand. In one we can seek lessons for the present in an instrumental view of the past. That approach suggests the might-have-beens of history. If only Communists had behaved differently; if nonsectarian radicals had pursued the proper policies; if the militant rank and file had been aware of its true interests (as distinguished from the false consciousness inculcated by trade union bureaucrats and New Deal Democrats); then the history of the 1930s would have been different and *better* [citing three works by the present author]. The second approach to our turbulent decade has been suggested by David Brody. 'The

interesting questions,' writes Brody, 'are not in the realm of what might have been, but in a closer examination of what did happen.' Brody's approach, I believe, promises greater rewards for scholars and may even be more useful for those who desire to use the past to improve the present and shape the future.'" Melvyn Dubofsky, "Not So 'Turbulent Years': A New Look at the 1930s," in *Life and Labor: Dimensions of Working Class History*, ed. Charles Stephenson and Robert Asher (Albany: State University of New York Press, 1986), 206. These comments miss the mark with regard to the present book, which consists precisely in a "closer examination of what did happen." Moreover, Brody himself has called on scholars unhappy with the current labor movement to set forth "the alternative that rivaled the union course that was actually taken." David Brody, "The CIO after 50 Years: A Historical Reckoning," *Dissent* 32 (Fall 1985): 470.

4. Gary Gerstle, *Working-Class Americanism: The Politics of Labor in a Textile City, 1914–1960* (Cambridge: Cambridge University Press, 1989), 165–66.

5. Michael K. Honey, *Southern Labor and Black Civil Rights: Organizing Memphis Workers* (Urbana: University of Illinois Press, 1993), 71, 99–103.

6. Elizabeth Faue, *Community of Suffering and Struggle: Women, Men, and the Laboring Movement in Minneapolis, 1915–1945* (Chapel Hill: University of North Carolina Press, 1991), 4. For solidarity unionism, see Staughton Lynd, *Solidarity Unionism: Rebuilding the Labor Movement from Below* (Chicago: Charles H. Kerr, 1992).

7. Gerstle, *Working-Class Americanism*, 143, 145; John Borsos, "Ironing Out Chaos: The CIO-ization of the United Rubber Workers, 1933–1941," unpublished manuscript, 13–14; Michael Kozura, "We Stood Our Ground: Anthracite Miners and the Expropriation of Corporate Property, 1930–1941," herein. [See also the account of UE organizer Mia Giunta concerning sharing work equally during layoffs at a Connecticut manufacturing plant in the 1970s, in *Rank and File: Personal Histories by Working-Class Organizers*, ed. Alice Lynd and Staughton Lynd, expanded ed. (Chicago: Haymarket Books, 2011), 330.]

8. John Borsos, "'We Make You This Appeal in the Name of Every Union Man and Woman in Barberton': Solidarity Unionism in Barberton, Ohio, 1933–41," herein.

9. See, for example, Daniel Nelson, *American Rubber Workers and Organized Labor, 1900–1941* (Princeton, NJ: Princeton University Press, 1988), 116–17 (factory council), 117–69 (federal labor unions); Ronald Edsforth, *Class Conflict and Cultural Consensus: The Making of a Mass Consumer Society in Flint, Michigan* (New Brunswick, NJ: Rutgers University Press, 1987), 130–36 (strike committee of 120 members), 162 (citywide council of federal labor unions), 181–83 (in the aftermath of the Flint sit-down, the UAW acts as a "general workers union," organizing bus drivers, department store clerks, taxi drivers, etc.).

10. Rosemary Feurer, "The Nutpickers' Union, 1933–34: Crossing the Boundaries of Community and Workplace," herein (in St. Louis the ability to build community mobilizations was the key to working-class strike success); Gerstle, *Working-Class Americanism*, chap. 4, "Citywide Mobilization,

1934–1936."

11. See Staughton Lynd, "The Possibility of Radicalism in the Early 1930s: The Case of Steel," in *Workers' Struggles Past and Present: A "Radical America" Reader*, ed. James Green (Philadelphia: Temple University Press, 1983), 191–92, 205n6 and n11.

12. Nelson, *American Rubber Workers*, 145. Sidney Hillman told his biographer, Mathew Josephson, that during the NRA period over 40,000 rubber workers had been organized. David Brody, "The Emergence of Mass-Production Unionism," in *Workers in Industrial America: Essays on the Twentieth Century Struggle* (New York: Oxford University Press, 1980), 90.

13. Edsforth, *Class Conflict*, 162, 265n11, 176.

14. Janet Irons, "The Challenge of National Coordination: Southern Textile Workers and the General Textile Strike of 1934," herein.

15. Kozura, "We Stood Our Ground."

16. Len DeCaux, *The Living Spirit of the Wobblies* (New York: International Publishers, 1978), 143.

17. Edsforth, *Class Conflict*, 159 (Klasey); Shelton Stromquist, *Solidarity and Survival: An Oral History of Iowa Labor in the Twentieth Century* (Iowa City: University of Iowa Press, 1993), 40, 115 (Ellis and the IUAW); Stan Weir, "Unions with Leaders Who Stay on the Job," herein (Blackie and Chips); John W. Anderson, "How I Became Part of the Labor Movement," in *Rank and File*, ed. Lynd and Lynd, 35, 61–62, 65; Steve Nelson with James R. Barrett and Rob Ruck, *Steve Nelson: American Radical* (Pittsburgh: University of Pittsburgh Press, 1981), 91–92 (Freeman Thompson).

18. David Montgomery, *The Fall of the House of Labor: The Workplace, the State, and American Labor Activism* (Cambridge: Cambridge University Press, 1987), 457.

19. Ibid., 322 (committee), 319 (IWW).

20. Ronald W. Schatz, *The Electrical Workers: A History of Labor at General Electric and Westinghouse, 1923–60* (Urbana: University of Illinois Press, 1983), 73.

21. "Workplace contractualism" is offered by David Brody to characterize "the essential characteristics of the union workplace regime that emerged out of the great New Deal organizing era in the mass-production sector of American industry." Brody, "Workplace Contractualism in Comparative Perspective," in *Industrial Democracy in America: The Ambiguous Promise*, ed. Nelson Lichtenstein and Howell John Harris (Cambridge: Cambridge University Press, 1993), 176.

22. Woods explains: "We said if you have a closed shop and check-off, everybody sits on their butts and they don't have to worry about organizing and they don't care what happens. We never wanted it." Sylvia Woods, "You Have to Fight for Freedom," in *Rank and File*, ed. Lynd and Lynd, 126. The organizers my wife and I interviewed for *Rank and File* told us that the advent of the dues check-off was the single most important cause of the bureaucratization of the CIO. Hence our generalization: "Once unions gained recognition and union dues were automatically taken out of the worker's paycheck, unions took on a new character." Ibid., 4.

23. Daniel Nelson, "Origins of the Sit-Down Era: Worker Militancy and Innovation in the Rubber Industry, 1934–1938," in *The Labor History Reader*, ed. Daniel J. Leab (Urbana: University of Illinois Press, 1985), 344.

24. Borsos, "Ironing Out Chaos," 20, 25–26, citing among other sources Donald Anthony, "Rubber Products: With a Specific Reference to the Akron Area," in *How Collective Bargaining Works: A Survey of Experience in Leading American Industries*, ed. Harry A. Mills (New York: Twentieth Century Fund, 1942), 654: "Although Goodrich was willing by April 1937 to come to an agreement, the first contract was not signed until May 27, 1938. [Local union leaders] felt that unless all demands were won, an agreement would so restrict freedom of action that it would not be worth while."

25. For John Sargent's assessment, see "Your Dog Don't Bark No More," above. Scholars support his appraisal. After examining the grievance committee minutes at Inland Steel during the late 1930s, and quoting from the accounts of Sargent and committeeman Nick Migas in *Rank and File*, Lizabeth Cohen states that "at steel mills where the SWOC did not yet have contracts and hence could not control the rank and file, shop floor agitation persisted." *Making a New Deal: Industrial Workers in Chicago, 1919–1939* (Cambridge: Cambridge University Press, 1990), 306–07.

26. Brody, "The Emergence of Mass-Production Unionism," 103.

27. Edsforth, *Class Conflict*, 171; Germer is quoted in Sidney Fine, *Sitdown: The General Motors Strike of 1936–1937* (Ann Arbor: University of Michigan Press, 1969), 136.

28. Edsforth, *Class Conflict*, 171. Louis Adamic, *My America, 1918–1938* (New York: Harper and Brothers, 1938), 414.

29. See Feurer, "The Nutpickers' Union," and Mark Naison, "The Southern Tenant Farmers' Union and the CIO," herein. According to Robin D. G. Kelley, *Hammer and Hoe: Alabama Communists during the Great Depression* (Chapel Hill: University of North Carolina Press, 1990), 143–44, Communists Joe Howard and C. Dave Smith organized a successful sit-down at the American Casting Company in 1936, only to be fired by the SWOC for acting without authorization.

30. At the Westinghouse plant near Pittsburgh, a key organizer was dismissed and 2,000 men and women walked off the job. By the next morning 13,000 striking workers had linked hands to form a huge human chain around the Westinghouse complex. Giant processions of strikers and supporters gradually closed down the entire Monongahela Valley. On November 1, 1916, a parade, bedecked with red flags and led by a Lithuanian band, invaded steel mills, chain works, and machinery companies, bringing out 36,000 workers. Montgomery, *Fall of the House of Labor*, 322–25. The Lawrence strike of 1919 is described in *The Essays of A. J. Muste*, ed. Nat Hentoff (New York: Macmillan, 1967), 55–77.

31. Walker C. Smith, "The Voyage of the Verona," in *Rebel Voices: An IWW Anthology*, ed. Joyce Kornbluh (Oakland: PM Press, 2011), 108.

32. Franklin Folsom, *Impatient Armies of the Poor: The Story of Collective Action of the Unemployed, 1808–1942* (Boulder: University of Colorado Press, 1991), 305.

33. Len DeCaux (before he went to work for the CIO) paraphrasing Lewis's testimony, Federated Press dispatch, Columbia University Oral History Project, April 2, 1935, quoted in "Possibility of Radicalism," above.

34. Ronald Radosh, "The Myth of the New Deal," in *A New History of Leviathan*, ed. R. Radosh and M. Rothbard (New York: E. P. Dutton, 1972), 152.

35. Brody, "The Emergence of Mass-Production Unionism," 103–04.

36. David Brody, "John L. Lewis," in *Workers in Industrial America*, 169–70.

37. William Forbath, *Law and the Shaping of the American Labor Movement* (Cambridge: Harvard University Press, 1991), 165.

38. Baldwin to Perkins, June 2, 1933, quoted in Cletus Daniel, *The American Civil Liberties Union and the Wagner Act: An Inquiry into the Depression-Era Crisis of American Liberalism* (Ithaca: Cornell University Press, 1980), 34.

39. Van Kleeck to Wagner, March 12, 1934, quoted in ibid., 71–73.

40. Baldwin to Walsh, March 20, 1934, quoted in ibid., 75; Baldwin to Wagner, April 1, 1935, quoted in ibid., pp. 101–02. [Senator Wagner, sponsor of the National Labor Relations Act, and Leon Keyserling, principal draftsperson of the statute, had similar apprehensions. In an interview conducted on March 2–3, 1986, a year and a half before his death, Keyserling explained why Section 13 of the NLRA contained remarkably explicit language seeking to protect the right to strike:

> There was a definite reason. First, because Wagner was always strong for the right to strike on the ground that without the right to strike, which was labor's ultimate weapon, they really had no other weapon. That guarantee was a part of his thinking. It was particularly necessary because a lot of people made the argument that because the government was giving labor the right to bargain collectively, that was a substitute for the right to strike, which was utterly wrong.

Kenneth M. Casebeer, "Holder of the Pen: An Interview with Leon Keyserling on Drafting the Wagner Act," *University of Miami Law Review* 42, No. 2 (November 1987): 353.]

41. Irons, "The Challenge of National Coordination."

42. Nelson, *American Rubber Workers*, 156.

43. C. J. Francis to Francis Biddle, January 10, 1935, Federal and Mediation Service Files, #170-1252, National Archives, Suitland Records Branch, Suitland, Maryland, quoted in Borsos, "We Make You This Appeal."

44. Peter Rachleff, "Organizing 'Wall to Wall': The Independent Union of All Workers, 1933–37," herein.

45. In the spring of 1934, 25 percent of all industrial workers belonged to company unions, with two-thirds of these organized under NRA auspices. Rick Fantasia, *Cultures of Solidarity: Consciousness, Action, and Contemporary American Workers* (Berkeley: University of California Press, 1988), 36–37. For company towns, see Eric Davin, "The Littlest New Deal: SWOC Takes Power in Steeltown," paper delivered at the annual meeting of the Organization of American Historians, 1992.

46. Lynd, "Possibility of Radicalism," above.

47. Borsos, "We Make You This Appeal" (the Diamond Match strike in 1934, the

Columbia Chemical strike in 1934, the Ohio Insulator strike in 1935, the Columbia Chemical sit-down strike in 1936, and the Pittsburgh Valve and Fittings strike in 1936).

48. Irons, "The Challenge of National Coordination," herein.
49. Janet Irons, "A New Deal for Labor? Southern Cotton Mill Workers and the General Strike of 1934," paper delivered at the annual meeting of the Organization of American Historians, 1989.
50. Brody, "The Emergence of Mass-Production Unionism," 104.
51. Edsforth, *Class Conflict*, 187, 272n101.
52. "Your Dog Don't Bark No More," above.
53. Ronald W. Schatz uses this phrase to describe unions as they were after the passage of the Taft-Hartley Act in 1947. "Philip Murray," in *Labor Leaders in America*, ed. Melvyn Dubofsky and Warren Van Tine (Urbana: University of Illinois Press, 1948), 250. But the words apply equally well to the status of unions certified by the NLRB as exclusive bargaining representatives at all times after the passage of the NLRA in 1935. As David Montgomery writes of the work of Secretary of Labor William B. Wilson during World War I: "The consistent theme guiding Wilson's work was that employers should be encouraged to negotiate with legitimate unions and to shun the IWW and other groups deemed 'outlaw' by the AFL. Here was the appearance in embryonic form of the doctrine of a certified bargaining agent, which was to be incorporated into the law of the land in 1935." Montgomery, *Fall of the House of Labor*, 357.
54. As Christopher Tomlins has most fully explicated, CIO unions surrendered their autonomy in exchange for government assistance in obtaining employer recognition. In fact, he writes, "the legitimacy of collective activity putatively guaranteed by labor relations law had been conditional almost from the outset. During the debates of the 1930s, proponents of the Wagner Act had stressed, both before and after its passage, that collective bargaining was a means to an end, and that the end was industrial stability and labor peace." The upshot was that "what the state offered workers and their organizations was ultimately no more than the opportunity to participate in the construction of their own subordination." *The State and the Unions: Labor Relations, Law, and the Organized Labor Movement in America, 1880–1960* (Cambridge: Cambridge University Press, 1986), 318, 327.
55. Not until 1943, twelve years after its founding, did the Independent Textile Union hire its first full-time organizers. Gerstle, *Working-Class Americanism*, 81–82, 269–70.
56. Cohen, *Making a New Deal*, 358.
57. Edsforth, *Class Conflict*, 182–83.
58. Steve Fraser, *Labor Will Rule: Sidney Hillman and the Rise of American Labor* (New York: Free Press, 1991), 403, and "The Labor Question," in *The Rise and Fall of the New Deal Order, 1930–1980*, ed. Steve Fraser and Gary Gerstle (Princeton: Princeton University Press, 1989), 77–78. Ronald Edsforth says substantially the same thing about the UAW's efforts to control shop direct action. Edsforth, *Class Conflict*, 177–78.
59. Irons, "Challenge of National Coordination."

60. Eric Leif Davin and Staughton Lynd, "Picket Line and Ballot Box: The Forgotten Legacy of the Local Labor Party Movement, 1932–1936," *Radical History Review* 22 (Winter 1979–1980): 43–63; Davin, "The Very Last Hurrah? The Defeat of the Labor Party Idea, 1934–1936," herein, and "The Littlest New Deal."

61. Steve Fraser, "Sidney Hillman: Labor's Machiavelli," in *Labor Leaders in America*, ed. Dubofsky and Van Tine, 221.

62. Fine, *Sitdown*, 90–91, characterizes the resolution to support a farmer-labor party as "a Communist party-line resolution." However, Kevin Boyle, "Building the Vanguard: Walter Reuther and Radical Politics in 1936," *Labor History* 30 (Summer 1989): 433–88, quotes at length from letters by Walter Reuther to his brothers Victor and Roy Reuther, April 22 and May 2, 1936, suggesting that Walter Reuther, a member of the Socialist Party at the time, strongly supported the resolution in favor of a farmer-labor third party and was aware of the many attempts to set up farmer-labor parties throughout the country.

63. David Brody, "The Uses of Power II: Political Action," quoting Philip Murray, in *Workers in Industrial America*, 220–21.

64. We agree with a great deal that is said in Frances Fox Piven and Richard A. Cloward, *Poor People's Movements: Why They Succeed, How They Fail* (New York: Pantheon, 1977), 96–180. However, these authors believe that workers scored their greatest triumphs in the 1930s "before they were organized into unions." Our view is that workers organized unions in the early 1930s but they were primarily local unions which differed qualitatively from the United Mine Workers and other national CIO unions.

65. John Borsos, "Talking Union: The Labor Movement in Barberton, Ohio, 1891–1991," PhD dissertation, Indiana University, 1992.

66. Phil Kwik, "Bargaining Pool Collapses at International Paper," *Labor Notes*, June 1992.

67. Lynd, *Solidarity Unionism*, 35 (Anna Walentynowicz quote); Roman Laba, *The Roots of Solidarity* (Princeton: Princeton University Press, 1991), chaps. 2 and 3, especially 66–67 (elected workplace committee at Warski shipyard), 68–69 (interfactory strike committee), and chap. 5, especially 106–12 (Walesa), 112 (horizontal structures).

68. Gerald Schlabach, "The Nonviolence of Desperation: Peasant Land Action in Honduras," in *Relentless Persistence: Nonviolent Action in Latin America*, ed. Philip McManus and Gerald Schlabach (Philadelphia: New Society, 1991), 66.

Afterword

1. A magnificent account of the broader movement from below that preceded the campaigns described in these pages is now available as chapter 10 of the new edition of Jeremy Brecher's book *Strike!* (PM Press). See also the comprehensive essay by Steve Early, "Saving Our Unions: Dare to Struggle, Dare to Win?," *Monthly Review*, February 2014. The factual descriptions that follow are based on a large number of newspaper and magazine articles. Among them are "Walmart Warehouse Strike Bolstered by Big Rally," *UE*

News, Autumn 2012; Dave Moberg, "En Masse and Without Precedent, Walmart Workers Rise Up," *In These Times*, October 11, 2012; Jake Olzen, "Why Direct Action Is Working for Walmart Workers," *Waging Non-Violence*, October 20, 2012; Matthew Cunningham-Cook, "How Workers Are Using Globalization against Walmart," *Portside*, October 24, 2012; Steven Greenhouse and Stephanie Clifford, "Protests Backed by Union Get Wal-Mart's Attention," *New York Times*, November 19, 2012; Jake Olzen, "How the Walmart Labor Struggle Is Going Global," *Waging Non-Violence*, January 15, 2013; Dave Kingman, "Walmart: Black Friday and Beyond," *Against the Current*, January/February 2013; Jenny Brown, "After a Pause, Walmart Strikes Back," *Labor Notes*, July 29, 2013; Steven Greenhouse, "Strike for Day Seeks to Raise Fast Food Pay," *New York Times*, August 1, 2013; Josh Eidelson, "Fast Food Strikes to Massively Expand," *Salon*, August 14, 2013; Harold Meyerson, "For Retailers, Low Wages Aren't Working Out," *Washington Post*, August 21, 2013; David Moberg, "Even without Unions, Wal-Mart Warehouse Empoyees Win Change," *In These Times*, August 21, 2013; Dennis Raj, "Fast Food Workers Standing Up for Themselves—and for Us," *Labor's Edge*, August 23, 2013; Labor Radio, "Warehouse Workers Fired for Taking Heat Breaks," August 25, 2013; Heather Somerville, "East Bay Fast-Food Workers to Strike Thursday," *Contra Costa Times*, August 27, 2013; Jean Tepperman, "Unionists and Other Supporters Back Fast Food Strikers," *East Bay Express*, August 31, 2013; Ned Resnikoff, "Among the Poorest Paid, a New Labor Revival," *MSNBC*, September 2, 2013; Josh Eidelson, "Protesting Activists' Firings, Walmart Workers Plan the Biggest Mobilization since Black Friday," *The Nation* blogs, September 3, 2013; "Pay Stagnation Births New Labor Movement," *USA Today*, September 6, 2013; Ryan Hill, "Opportunities Present for 'Labor Left' in Walmart and Fast Food Fights," *Solidarity*, October 9, 2013; "Three Stories about Walmart," *Portside*, November 18, 2013; Steven Greenhouse, "On Register's Other Side, Little Money to Spend," *New York Times*, November 29, 2013.

2. David Moberg, "The Walmart Revolt: New Strategies for Old Labor," *In These Times*, January 2013.

3. In December 2013 a letter from Robin Alexander, UE director of international affairs, to "Union Sisters and Brother, Activists, and Friends" asserted that Warehouse Workers for Justice (WWJ), the entity that conducted the Elwood struggle, had "recovered over $1 million in stolen wages and benefits, improved safety conditions, and helped workers secure higher wages." She added that WWJ had expanded its work to additional warehouses in the Walmart supply chain.

4. Robert M. Schwartz, "Working without a Contract: A Strategy Whose Time Has Come?," *Labor Notes*, February 15, 2003.

5. Arun Gupta, "Fight for 15 Confidential," *In These Times*, November 11, 2013, reprinted by *Portside*, November 16, 2013. And see, in general agreement, Erik Forman, "Fast Food Unionism: The Unionization of McDonald's and the McDonaldization of Unions," *Industrial Worker*, December 2013.

6. Staughton Lynd and Daniel Gross, *Labor Law for the Rank and Filer: Building Solidarity While Staying Clear of the Law*, 2nd ed. (Oakland: PM Press,

2011), and *Solidarity Unionism at Starbucks* (Oakland: PM Press, 2011).

7. Elizabeth A. Harris, "Labor Panel Finds Illegal Punishments at Walmart," *New York Times*, November 19, 2013.

8. Sylvia Woods, "You Have to Fight for Freedom," in *Rank and File: Personal Histories by Working-Class Organizers*, ed. Alice Lynd and Staughton Lynd, expanded ed. (Chicago: Haymarket Books, 2011), 126.

9. Stella Nowicki, "Back of the Yards," in ibid., 87.

10. Charles J. Morris, *The Blue Eagle at Work: Reclaiming Democratic Rights in the American Workplace* (Ithaca: Cornell University Press, 2005), and "Members-Only Collective Bargaining: Get Ready for an Old Concept with a New Use," http://charlesjmorris.blogspot.com/, reprinted in *Portside*, August 3, 2013.

11. A CBS News poll of 1,010 Americans, done November 15–18, 2013, found that 69 percent of respondents approved of raising the federal minimum wage. This majority included 57 percent of Republicans as well as higher percentages of Democrats and independents. A study by BigInsights Monthly Consumer Survey found that nearly two-fifths of Walmart customers, nearly half of Kmart customers, and a little more than a quarter of those who shop at Target have household incomes below $35,000. Thus an increase in minimum wage might be desirable for employers by increasing the amount of money spent on a company's products and services by its own employees. A number of state and local jurisdictions have enacted laws mandating a minimum wage higher than that currently required by federal law. Greenhouse, "On Register's Other Side."

Index

Also available from Haymarket Books

Rank and File
Personal Histories by Working-Class Organizers
(Updated and expanded edition)
By Staughton Lynd

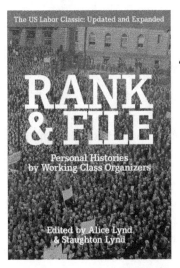

"One of the best works of oral history produced by radical historians. . . . For readers who want to see an alternative view to social trade union history, in which labor leaders take the center stage, *Rank and File* is the place to begin."
—*Nation*

The activity of the rank-and-file organizers in this book covers the 1930s—1960s, and with the addition of accounts from The New Rank and File, the 1970s—1990s. Brought to life in their own words, in this vibrant collection of oral histories, they were each militant in demanding changes in their unions, workplaces, and society at large.

Order online at
HaymarketBooks.org

About the Author

Staughton Lynd received a BA from Harvard, an MA and PhD from Columbia, and a JD from the University of Chicago. He taught American history at Spelman College in Atlanta, where one of his students was the future Pulitzer Prize—winning novelist Alice Walker, and at Yale University. Staughton served as director of Freedom Schools in the Mississippi Summer Project of 1964. He has written or edited numerous books, including *Rank and File: Personal Histories by Working-Class Organizers*, ed. Alice and Staughton Lynd, expanded ed. (Chicago: Haymarket Books, 2011).

9 781608 463886